Christmas Is Coming

Appliqué Quilt Patterns to Celebrate the Season

Cheryl Almgren Taylor

Martingale®
Create with Confidence

Dedication

To my grandsons, Taylor Kline, Michael Kline, Ryan Kline, Cale Sweeney, and Noah Taylor, and my son, Jeff Taylor, with memories of happy Christmases past.

Christmas Is Coming: Appliqué Quilt Patterns
to Celebrate the Season
© 2013 by Cheryl Almgren Taylor

Martingale®
19021 120th Ave. NE, Ste. 102
Bothell, WA 98011-9511 USA
ShopMartingale.com

Printed in China
18 17 16 15 14 13   8 7 6 5 4 3 2 1

Library of Congress Cataloging-in-Publication Data is available upon request.

ISBN: 978-1-60468-198-7

MISSION STATEMENT
Dedicated to providing quality products and service to inspire creativity.

CREDITS
President and CEO: Tom Wierzbicki
Editor in Chief: Mary V. Green
Design Director: Paula Schlosser
Managing Editor: Karen Costello Soltys
Acquisitions Editor: Karen M. Burns
Technical Editor: Laurie Baker
Copy Editor: Tiffany Mottet
Production Manager: Regina Girard
Cover and Interior Designer: Regina Girard
Illustrator: Rose Sheifer
Photographer: Brent Kane

Contents

Introduction

Christmas is my favorite holiday and brings to mind memories of childhood and happy times with friends of the past and present.

It fills me with joy, goodwill, and the desire to give everyone I love a special quilt. In addition to the time and effort that goes into making a quilt, there's a piece of my heart as well. At Christmastime, I always want to share this special part of my life with others, and so this book is filled with projects that share a part of me with you.

As I created the designs for this book, I tried to provide a little something for many types of quilters. For those procrastinators that need a fast project, the "Rejoice Wall Hanging" (page 88) sews up quickly, as does the "Welcome Wall Hanging" (page 16), a favorite of mine because its simple church building bears a striking resemblance to the church my husband pastors. There are also a variety of table runners that are one- or two-day projects, including "First Day of Christmas Table Runner" (page 24), "Christmas Ornaments Table Runner" (page 66), "Candy Canes Table Runner" (page 75), and "Glad Tidings Table Runner" (page 84).

I've also tried to provide projects that aren't fast and easy, but special and unique. For those who want elegance and sparkle, "Christmas Bouquet Wall Hanging" (page 48) is perfect for a traditional quilt with an heirloom feel. The "Night Before Christmas Quilt" (page 56) is designed for people like me who love appliqué and the stories it allows us to create. The whimsical "Christmas Pageant Wall Hanging" (page 42) makes me smile, with its group of child-performers who were inspired by my own grandchildren.

If you're looking for a gift idea besides the usual quilt or table runner, there's a card holder, a pillow, and a bed runner as well. The "Christmas Greetings Card Holder" (page 38) is useful as well as decorative, and sews up in a day. The "Keeping Watch O'er Their Flocks Pillow" (page 80) is also fast to make and a great last-minute gift idea. And for those who want to decorate their bedroom but don't have time to create a bed-sized Christmas quilt, the "Home for Christmas Bed Runner" (page 28) is much less effort and so much fun. The snow-covered trees and quaint village scene evoke memories of Christmas past with a Norman Rockwell flavor.

I hope this collection of Christmas designs speaks to your heart and you find a special project, or two, that will add to the joy and excitement of the holiday season. I hope your home is filled with the peace and love that's the reason for the season. It's time to rejoice and be glad. Christmas is coming!

~Cheryl

Quiltmaking Tools and Supplies

Having the right equipment for the job, whether you're creating a quilt or building a house, makes the entire experience quicker and more pleasant.

Fabric

The fabric of choice for quilting has traditionally been 100% cotton. It's my personal recommendation to all quilters. Today we can find cotton in a huge variety of prints and styles, even with metallic elements.

When selecting specific prints for a project, I often use tone-on-tone or batik fabrics. Batiks are wonderful because they allow you to include shading in your appliqué pieces with no extra effort except careful placement. I also use small-scale prints that read as solids to provide additional interest. I seldom use solids because of their lack of visual texture.

Thread

When using the fusible-web appliqué technique and finishing your edges with a machine blanket stitch or other decorative stitch, thread becomes an important element in your quilt design—just as important as your fabric. You should understand that thread comes in different weights, and the larger the weight number, the thinner and finer the thread. Therefore, 100-weight thread is very fine and 25-weight thread is extremely thick. The thread weight will also impact the size and type of needle you want to use.

While I've heard many quilt designers state that they always use a certain brand or type of thread, I find that one thread doesn't fit all needs. I prefer several different types of thread for different parts of the quiltmaking process.

I like to use a 60-weight or a 2-ply 50-weight thread for piecing. These weights will give you less bulk in your seams and a truer block size. I also like these weights of thread for quilting, or I use 100-weight silk thread. It gives a beautiful look to the quilt top and keeps the quilt soft and pliable, even with very intricate, heavy quilting.

My signature technique is fusible-web appliqué and that involves finishing the raw edges of appliqué pieces with a machine blanket stitch. In most instances I want my thread to blend into the background. To accomplish this, my favorite thread is 3-ply 50-weight in a matching color. It's a nice weight and doesn't overpower the design. However, the blanket stitch on different machines can vary. My machine does a single stitch when it sews the blanket stitch, but some machines double stitch, making a very thick edging. If that's the case with your machine, a 3-ply 50-weight thread may be too bulky and overpower the design. You may want to use a 60-weight or a 2-ply 50-weight thread to accommodate this extra stitching. You can even experiment with a 100-weight silk thread.

Sometimes you want your thread to become a strong design element, adding glitz and glamour to your project. On those occasions, I often use rayon thread with a sheen or even metallic thread. Many of the quilts in this book had a little extra glitter provided by gold metallic thread.

Sewing-Machine Needles

Needles are sized with two numbers, such as 80/12 (European/American), and sizing is the reverse of thread size—the larger the number, the larger the needle. The larger the needle, the larger the hole made as it punctures the quilt top. Using the right needle will make a huge improvement in the quality of the finished quilt and your happiness with the entire quilting process.

I use Sharp needles for piecing, embroidery needles for finishing appliqué edges, and quilting needles for quilting (of course). I usually use a size 75/11 needle, but a size 70/10 or 80/12 can also be a good choice depending on the thread you're using. Choose the smallest needle that works with your thread so the thread fills the hole and doesn't leave a visible opening. I never use universal needles for piecing or quilting because they have rounded tips that don't produce the nice, even stitches that Sharps do.

Specialty needles are designed for different types of threads and different purposes. Metallic threads require the use of a metallic needle if you want a happy sewing experience. Metallic needles are designed with an extra-large eye and will reduce the fraying and breaking that's sometimes a problem when using metallic thread. The smallest metallic needle I recommend is 80/12, but 90/14 is also a common size. For machine quilting, use needles specifically created for machine quilting; they're designed to go through several layers of fabric and sew evenly over seams.

Change your needles often as you're working. A dull needle tip will make sewing difficult and create problems with your stitch. I shudder to think back to when I first began to sew and never changed my needle unless it broke! I've learned my lesson since then.

Quiltmaking Techniques

This section will cover all the techniques needed to make the quilts in this book.

Rotary Cutting

Rotary cutting requires several tools. These include a rotary cutter, cutting mat, 24"-long acrylic ruler, and a small square ruler.

Cutting Straight-Grain Strips

1. Iron your fabric to remove any wrinkles. Fold it in half with the selvage edges together and lay it on the cutting mat, aligning the folded edge with a horizontal line on the mat. On the left edge of the fabric, place the square ruler along the fold and butt the 24"-long ruler against the left edge of the square so that it covers ¼" to ½" of the raw edges.

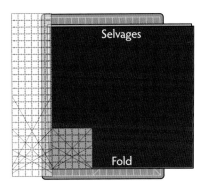

2. Holding the long ruler firmly in place with your left hand, remove the small ruler. Roll the rotary cutter along the right edge of the ruler across the width of the fabric. Never cut toward yourself; always cut away. Discard the uneven scrap. This is called "clean cutting" and leaves you with a straight edge from which to cut your strips.

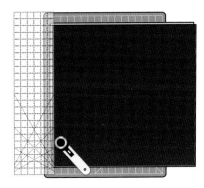

3. Align the ruler at the desired measurement along the edge of the fabric. Make sure that the ruler marking is on top of the fabric edge and not beside it, which would make your fabric strip too narrow. Cut along the ruler edge toward the selvage. Repeat the process for the necessary amount of strips.

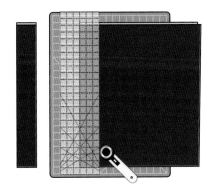

4. After cutting several strips, it may be necessary to straighten the fabric edge again. If so, repeat steps 1 and 2, and then continue cutting the required number of strips.

5. Squares and rectangles can now be cut from the strips. Trim away the selvage ends of the folded strips. Measure the required distance from the straightened ends of the strip and cut the pieces. You'll be cutting two pieces at once.

Cutting Bias Strips

1. To cut bias strips, open up your fabric and lay it flat on your cutting mat, right side up. Align the 45° line on your rotary cutting ruler with the bottom selvage edge. Cut along the ruler edge to make the first cut.

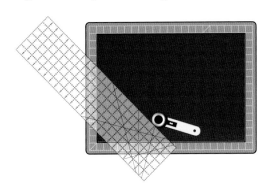

❷ Using the first cut as a guide, align the desired strip-width measurement on the ruler with the cut edge of the fabric. Cut along the edge of the ruler. Continue cutting strips until you have the quantity needed.

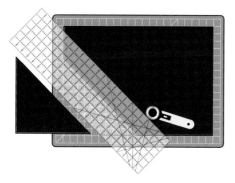

Fusible-Web Appliqué

The process of appliquéing, adding fabric shapes to the top of a background fabric, has been around for hundreds of years. Traditional appliqué is done by stitching the motifs in place by hand, but I prefer to use fusible-web appliqué, which differs from traditional methods in several ways.

One of the first things to consider when using fusible-web appliqué is that asymmetrical designs must be prepared in reverse, or as a mirror image, otherwise your finished design will be facing backward. *The designs in this book have already been reversed for you so you don't have to do this step.*

Preparing the Appliqué Pieces

There are a variety of fusible-web products on the market. I recommend a paper-backed, *lightweight* product. Be sure to read the manufacturer's instructions when applying fusible web to your fabric, because each brand is a little different and requires slightly different fusing times. Be aware that pressing too long may remove the adhesive and the piece won't stick well. In areas of high humidity, some products have problems with the paper backing separating from the fusible web. If this happens to you, I recommend trying a different brand.

❶ To prepare your pieces, begin by tracing the pattern directly onto the paper side of the fusible web. It's helpful to use a light box if you have one.

TRACING MULTIPLES

If you're tracing an appliqué shape that will need to be repeated multiple times, such as the leaves in "Christmas Bouquet Wall Hanging" (page 48), you may find it beneficial to use a template. For this method, trace the shape onto template plastic using a fine-tip permanent pen. Cut out the plastic shape exactly on the drawn line. Use this piece as a template and trace around it onto the paper side of the fusible web until you have drawn the required number of shapes. This will ensure that all your shapes are identical.

❷ After the shapes are drawn on the paper-backed fusible web, roughly cut out each shape, leaving about a ¼" margin outside the traced line. Do not cut on the traced line at this point. To reduce the stiffness in medium- or large-sized appliqué shapes, cut away the center portion of the paper-backed fusible web, being sure to leave at least a ¼" of paper inside the traced line. This is often called the "doughnut" technique.

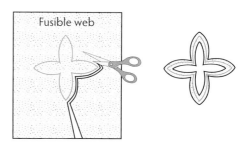

Fusible web

❸ Follow the manufacturer's instructions to fuse each shape to the wrong side of the appropriate fabric, and then cut out the shape on the traced line. Don't remove the paper backing until you're ready to fuse the shape in place.

Wrong side of fabric

Fusing Shapes to the Background

❶ When you are ready to fuse the appliqué shapes to the background fabric, remove the paper backing and position the shapes on the background in numerical order. A dotted line on a pattern indicates that a piece is underneath an adjacent piece. It's often helpful to use a placement guide for accuracy (see "Creating a Placement Guide" below).

CREATING A PLACEMENT GUIDE

A placement guide is a full-sized image of the finished appliqué that's placed either over or under the background piece and used to position each appliqué shape. Depending on the material selected for your placement guide, the placement guide may be used *over* the background piece if the fabric is dark colored or *under* the background piece if the fabric is light colored.

To make a placement guide, trace the pattern for the complete appliqué image from this book onto a see-through material. Because the patterns in this book are reversed for ease in making the fabric shapes, you'll need to reverse the pattern given to make the placement guide.

For an overlay placement guide, the best material to use is overhead transparency sheets. They come in styles that can be run through a copier or printer, making the appliqué shape construction very easy. Remember to slide the pieces underneath the transparency for placement and to remove the transparency before fusing the pieces in place.

Materials that work well for underlay placement guides include freezer paper, graph paper, and tracing paper. Medical paper used on examining tables is also a great product to use, as well as quilting paper.

❷ Once everything is placed correctly on the background fabric, fuse the pieces in place, referring to the manufacturer's instructions for temperature and time.

❸ Stitch around the edges of each appliqué piece using a machine blanket stitch, zigzag stitch, or satin stitch.

Preassembling Appliqué Units

When several appliqué pieces are needed to make the complete appliqué shape, such as the houses in "Home for Christmas Bed Runner" (page 28), it's helpful to preassemble the pieces into a unit before fusing to the background. A Teflon pressing sheet is very helpful for this because fusible web will not adhere to the sheet.

To preassemble an appliqué unit, prepare the shapes as instructed in "Preparing the Appliqué Pieces" (page 8). Lay the appliqué pieces on the pressing sheet in numerical order; use a placement guide if desired. Remove the paper backing behind the areas that overlap another appliqué shape, but not from the entire piece. Then fuse the pieces together. Keep the rest of the paper backing in place until you're ready to fuse the entire unit to the background fabric.

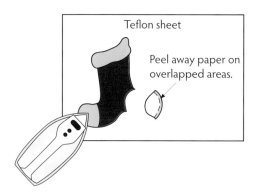

Teflon sheet

Peel away paper on overlapped areas.

Paper Piecing

Paper piecing is a method used in the border corner blocks of "Welcome Wall Hanging" (page 16). Although traditional piecing could be used for the same design, paper piecing makes it easier to handle the small pieces and also ensures accurate results.

It's possible to purchase paper specifically designed for paper piecing, but you can also use tracing paper, vellum paper, or medical exam-table paper. The paper needs to be easy to see through and tear away easily.

❶ Transfer the patterns onto your paper foundation and make the required number of copies of each unit. Be sure to transfer the numbers, which indicate the sewing order. Roughly cut around each foundation so that you can work on each one individually.

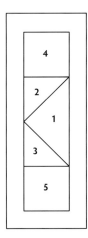

❷ Set the stitch length on your sewing machine to 15 to 18 stitches per inch. You may also wish to use a larger needle size, such as 90/14. The smaller stitch length and the larger needle will enable the paper to tear away easily when you're done.

❸ Working with one foundation pattern at a time, turn the foundation pattern so the marked side is facing up. Position the fabric piece specified in the instructions for area 1 over area 1 of the pattern, right side up, making sure it completely covers the area and extends ¼" past the lines on all sides. *When paper piecing, the fabric pieces must always extend at least ¼" past the lines, including those along the perimeter of the block. This is your seam-allowance fabric.*

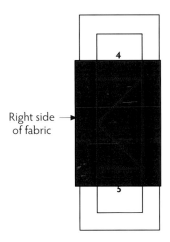

Right side of fabric

❹ Place the fabric piece for area 2 over area 2, making sure it completely covers the area and has an ample ¼" seam allowance on all sides. Flip it over on top of piece 1, right sides together, and pin it in place.

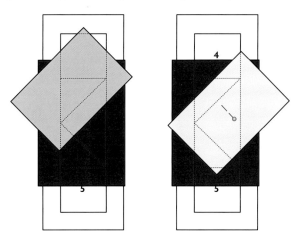

❺ Flip the foundation pattern over so that the *unmarked* side is on top. You should still be able to see the lines that are drawn on the other side. Position the unit under the presser foot, and sew exactly on the line between areas 1 and 2, starting and ending a few stitches past the line with a backstitch.

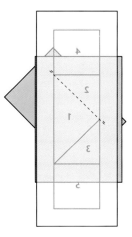

❻ Turn the paper over and open piece 2. Press the seam allowances to one side using a dry iron. Trim the seam allowance to ¼" if necessary, being careful not to cut into the paper. A ¼" seam allowance should extend into area 3. Place the selected fabric for area 3 over area 3, checking that it extends ¼" on all sides; flip it over onto piece 1 and pin it in place. Turn the foundation paper over and sew directly on the line between areas 1 and 3. Press the seam allowances to one side.

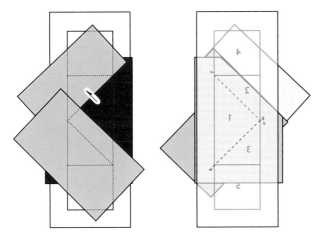

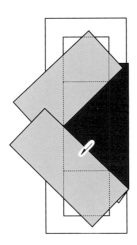

7 In numerical order, continue adding fabric pieces to each area until the unit is completed.

8 Trim the unit along the dashed lines, which should be ¼" from the solid lines.

9 Repeat steps 3–8 with each of the remaining foundations. After the blocks are assembled into the quilt top, you'll tear away the foundation paper. It's important to leave the foundation paper in place until your blocks are sewn to another piece, because some of the edges may be bias.

Squaring Up Blocks

The backgrounds of appliqué blocks are oversized to allow for some distortion that occurs while appliquéing. Before assembling the quilt, you'll need to trim the blocks to size.

1 Locate the center of the block, and then establish the midpoint of the block on a ruler. For example, on a block that is 8½" square, the midpoint of the block is 4¼" down from the top and 4¼" in from the side. (This is a small block; depending on the size of the block, you may need to use more than one ruler.)

2 Place the ruler on the block, aligning the center of the block and the midpoint on the ruler. Trim the excess fabric from one side.

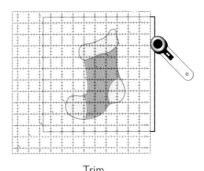

Trim.

3 Rotate the block and repeat step 2 for each of the remaining sides.

Adding Borders

Some of the quilts in this book have pieced borders; others have borders with butted corners. For pieced borders, follow the instructions given with the project. Follow the instructions below for borders with butted corners.

I recommend waiting to cut your borders until your quilt top is ready for them. Always measure through the center of the quilt when measuring for borders, because the sides of the quilt can easily become distorted during construction.

If your border is longer than 40", you'll need to piece the border strips to achieve the required length. When piecing border strips, use a diagonal seam. Trim the seam allowances to ¼" and press them open.

To add borders to your quilt:

1 Measure through the center of the quilt from top to bottom. Prepare two border strips to this measurement. Locate the center of the borders and the center of the quilt sides by folding them in half and finger-pressing to mark the centers. Matching centers and ends, pin the borders to each side of the quilt, right sides together. Sew using a ¼" seam allowance. Press the seam allowances toward the border.

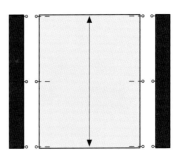

❷ Measure through the center of the quilt from side to side, including the side borders. Prepare two border strips to this measurement. Mark the center of the borders and center of the quilt top and bottom. Matching centers and ends, pin the borders to the top and bottom of the quilt, right sides together. Sew using a ¼" seam allowance. Press the seam allowances toward the border.

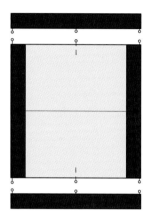

Binding

After the quilting is complete, you'll need to bind the quilt edges. Before you attach the binding, trim the batting and backing even with the quilt top and square up the quilt sandwich. Be sure the three layers of the quilt are basted together along the edges.

You'll encounter two types of angles on the projects in this book. Most of the quilt projects have square (or 90°) corners. However, "Christmas Ornaments Table Runner" (page 66) and "Glad Tidings Table Runner" (page 84) have corners with odd angles and will need to be treated differently.

Cutting and Joining Strips

❶ Cut your fabric strips the width specified in the project instructions, cutting across the width of the fabric from selvage to selvage.

❷ To join the strips, place the ends of two strips right sides together as shown. Sew diagonally across the strips. Trim the seam allowances to ¼" and press the seam allowances open. Join the remaining strips in the same manner to make one long strip.

❸ Press the binding strip in half lengthwise, wrong sides together and raw edges aligned.

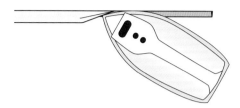

Binding Square Corners

❶ Beginning near the center of one edge, align the raw edges of the binding with the edge of the quilt top. Begin stitching about 8" from the end of the binding strip using a ¼" seam allowance. Stop sewing ¼" from the corner. Backstitch and remove the quilt from under the sewing machine.

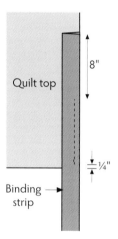

❷ Fold the binding up at a 90° angle so the fold forms a 45° angle. The binding edge should be aligned with the next side of the quilt.

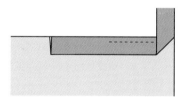

❸ Fold the binding back down on itself, leaving the 45° angle in place underneath. Align the binding and quilt edges and continue sewing, repeating the procedure at each corner.

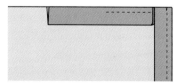

❹ When you're approximately 8" from the beginning of the binding, overlap the beginning and end of the binding strip. Trim the end so that the overlap measures 2½" (or the width of the binding strip).

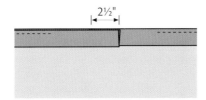

❺ Open the folded binding and place the two ends right sides together. Mark a diagonal line on the wrong side. Sew the ends together on the line. Check to make sure the binding fits the quilt edge, and then trim the seam allowances to ¼" and press them open. Refold the binding and finish sewing it in place.

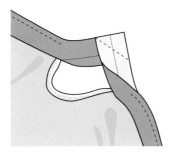

❻ Fold the binding over the edge of the quilt to the back. Hand stitch it in place, forming miters at the corners.

Binding Odd Angles

❶ Cut and join the binding strips as described in "Cutting and Joining Strips", opposite.

❷ Mark the sewing line along all of the edges of the project top. The intersection of the sewing lines will be clearly visible to you. When you're attaching the binding, the intersections will be stopping points.

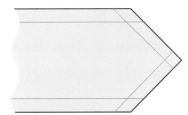

❸ Beginning near the center of one edge, align the raw edges of the binding with the edge of the quilt top. Begin stitching about 8" from the end of the

binding strip using a ¼" seam allowance. Stop at the angle intersection *exactly* on the intersection point. Backstitch and remove the quilt from under the sewing machine.

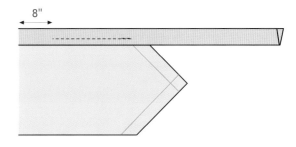

❹ Position the quilt so you're ready to stitch the next side. Fold up the binding so it extends straight up and is in line with the next side of the quilt.

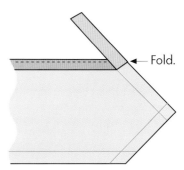

← Fold.

❺ Fold the binding back down on itself, leaving the angle in place underneath. Align the binding edge with the quilt edge and continue sewing until you reach the intersection at the end point of the quilt.

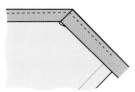

❻ The end point is a square corner and can be treated as such (see "Binding Square Corners", opposite). Once you've applied the binding to the point, continue sewing until you reach the intersection of the next odd angle and repeat the folding and stitching procedure. Continue around the quilt until all the corners have been bound. Refer to steps 4–6 of "Binding Square Corners" to complete the binding process.

Home for the Holidays

Part of the joy of the Christmas season is the preparation and anticipation of the day itself. Preparing gifts, decorating the house, and planning for the great event add excitement to the season. From the welcoming wall hanging in the entry way to the festive bed runner in the guest bedroom, from the tasteful table runner gracing the dining-room table to the attractive card holder in the den, quilts add warmth and beauty to your home. So, it's time to get ready . . . and come home for the holidays!

Welcome Wall Hanging

Finished wall hanging: 23½" x 29¾" • *Pieced and appliquéd by Cheryl Almgren Taylor. Quilted by Cheryl Winslow.*

*This quick and welcoming wall hanging will greet visitors during
the Christmas season and throughout the coming days of winter.*

Materials

Yardage is based on 42"-wide fabric.

⅝ yard of blue batik for background

⅝ yard of gold metallic print for letter appliqués, sashing, inner border, outer-border corner blocks, and binding

½ yard of red batik for outer border

¼ yard of white tone-on-tone print for church section background

¼ yard of cream batik for letter background

⅛ yard of gold metallic plaid for outer-border corner blocks

Scraps of assorted green, white, light-brown, dark-brown, yellow, and red fabrics for appliqués

1 yard of fabric for backing

27" x 33" piece of batting

½ yard of 17"-wide lightweight paper-backed fusible web

Assorted threads to match appliqué fabrics

Teflon pressing sheet (recommended)

Foundation paper for paper piecing

Orange Pigma Micron pen (optional)

Cutting

From the fusible web, cut:
- 1 strip, 1" x 17½"

From the white tone-on-tone print, cut:
- 1 rectangle, 4" x 17½"

From the blue batik, cut:
- 1 rectangle, 16½" x 17½"

From the cream batik, cut:
- 1 rectangle, 5" x 17½"

From the gold metallic print, cut:
- 3 strips, 1¼" x 42"; crosscut into:
    - 1 strip, 1¼" x 17"
    - 2 strips, 1¼" x 23¼"
    - 2 strips, 1¼" x 18½"
- 2 strips, 1½" x 42"; crosscut into 32 squares, 1½" x 1½"
- 3 strips, 2½" x 42"

From the red batik, cut:
- 3 strips, 3" x 42"; crosscut into:
    - 2 strips, 3" x 24¾"
    - 2 strips, 3" x 18"
- 16 rectangles, 1½" x 2"
- 16 squares, 1½" x 1½"

From the gold metallic plaid, cut:
- 4 squares, 2" x 2"

Creating the Center Panel

1. To make the background piece for the church section, apply the fusible-web strip along one long edge of the wrong side of the white rectangle. Do not remove the paper backing yet. Using the photo (page 16) as a reference, cut an undulating line along the long fused edge of the rectangle, being careful not to cut any deeper than the width of the fusible web.

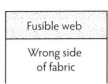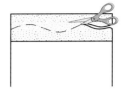

Fusible web

Wrong side of fabric

2. Remove the paper backing and overlap the fusible edge of the white rectangle approximately ¼" over the blue rectangle; fuse in place. The assembled unit should be at least 19" in length.

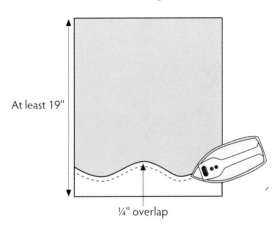

At least 19"

¼" overlap

3. Refer to "Fusible-Web Appliqué" (page 8) and use the patterns (pages 20–23) to prepare the individual appliqué pieces for the church and letter sections. Consult the materials list and the photo for fabric choices as needed. Preassemble the church and tree units using the prepared pieces (see "Preassembling Appliqué Units" on page 9).

4. Arrange the prepared appliqué unit on the background piece from step 2, placing the bottom of the church approximately 2¼" from the background lower edge. Follow the manufacturer's instructions to fuse the pieces in place, leaving at least ½" of space on each side for trimming and seam allowances.

⑤ For the letter section, center the letters on the cream rectangle; fuse in place.

⑥ Finish the raw edges of each appliqué piece using a machine blanket stitch, zigzag stitch, or satin stitch. Use a satin stitch to create the flame for each candle. You may want to experiment on some fabric scraps before stitching on the actual piece. Or you may wish to draw the flames with an orange Pigma Micron pen.

⑦ Trim the church section to 17" x 18½" and the letter section to 17" x 4½".

⑧ Sew the gold metallic print 1¼" x 17" strip to the bottom of the church section. Add the letter section to the bottom of the strip. Press the seam allowances toward the strip.

Paper Piecing the Outer-Border Corner Blocks

❶ Referring to "Paper Piecing" (page 9), make eight copies each of the side-points unit pattern and the top/bottom-points unit pattern (opposite). Using the red 1½" x 2" rectangles for piece 1 on both patterns, the gold metallic print 1½" squares for pieces 2 and 3 on both patterns, and the red 1½" squares for pieces 4 and 5 of the top/bottom-points pattern, paper piece the foundations.

❷ Sew completed side-points units to the sides of each gold metallic plaid 2" square. Press the seam allowances toward the squares. Join completed top/bottom-points units to the top and bottom of these units. Press the seam allowances toward the top/bottom-points units. The blocks should measure 3" x 3", including the ¼" seam allowances.

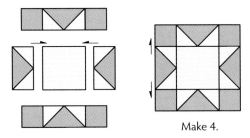

Make 4.

Assembling the Wall-Hanging Top

❶ Refer to the wall-hanging assembly diagram, opposite, to sew the gold metallic 1¼" x 23¼" strips to the sides of the wall-hanging top. Press the seam allowances toward the borders. Add the gold metallic 1¼" x 18½" strips to the top and bottom of the wall-hanging top. Press the seam allowances toward the borders. The wall hanging should measure 18½" x 24¾" in order for the outer border to fit.

2 Sew the red 3" x 24¾" strips to the sides of the wall-hanging top. Press the seam allowances toward the outer-border strips. Add a paper-pieced corner block to each end of the red 3" x 18½" strips. Press the seam allowances toward the strips. Join these strips to the top and bottom of the wall hanging. Press the seam allowances toward the outer-border strip

Wall-hanging assembly

Finishing the Wall Hanging

1 Prepare the backing so that it's 4" longer and 4" wider than the wall-hanging top.

2 Layer the backing, batting, and wall-hanging top; baste together.

3 Quilt as desired.

4 When the quilting is complete, square up the wall-hanging sandwich. Refer to "Binding" (page 12) to attach the binding using the gold metallic print 2½"-wide strips.

5 Add a hanging sleeve and a label to the back of the wall hanging.

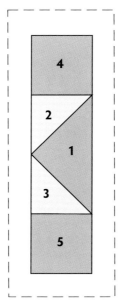

Top/bottom-points unit

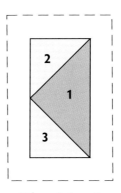

Side-points unit

Church section appliqué patterns and placement guide, section A

Patterns are reversed for fusible appliqué.

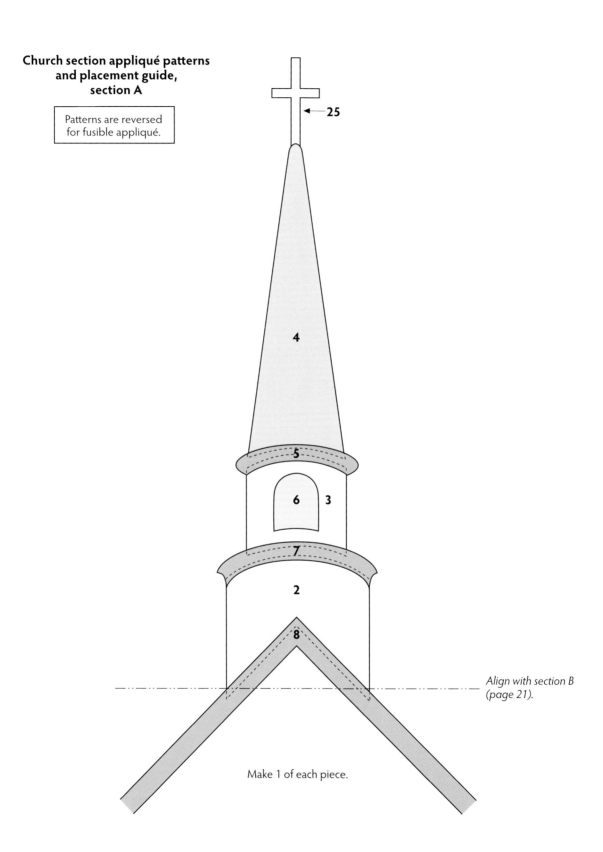

← 25

4

5

6 3

7

2

8

Align with section B (page 21).

Make 1 of each piece.

**Church section appliqué patterns
and placement guide,
section B**

Patterns are reversed
for fusible appliqué.

2

8

*Align with section A
(page 20).*

9

17

20

13

Make 1 of each piece.

1

16

10

24

23

18

11

21

19

14

22

12

15

Church section appliqué patterns and placement guide

Patterns are reversed
for fusible appliqué.

Make 1 and 1 reversed
of each piece.

Letter section appliqué patterns

Patterns are reversed
for fusible appliqué.

Make 2 of letter "e"
and 1 each
of remaining letters.

First Day of Christmas Table Runner

Finished table runner: 18½" x 42" • *Pieced and appliquéd by Cheryl Almgren Taylor. Quilted by Cheryl Winslow.*

Simple appliqué and easy piecing make this table runner a fast project that can be made in a weekend. The neutral and golden tones provide a warm backdrop for gracious dining. Add your own partridge, turtle doves, and even some French hens as table decorations!

Materials

Yardage is based on 42"-wide fabric.

⅝ yard *total* of assorted cream and tan fabrics for pieced center panel

½ yard of gold-metallic-on-black print for inner border and binding

½ yard of cream fabric for pieced outer border

⅜ yard of gold batik for pieced outer border

1 fat eighth of yellow batik for pear appliqués

1 fat eighth of green batik for holly appliqués

Scraps of assorted red fabrics for berry appliqués

Scrap of brown fabric for stem appliqués

1½ yards of fabric for backing

22" x 46" piece of batting

½ yard of 17"-wide lightweight paper-backed fusible web

Assorted threads to match appliqué fabrics

Teflon pressing sheet (recommended)

Cutting

From the assorted cream and tan fabrics, cut a *total* of:
- 48 squares, 3½" x 3½"

From the gold-metallic-on-black print, cut:
- 4 strips, 2½" x 42"
- 3 strips, 1½" x 42"; crosscut into:
  - 2 strips, 1½" x 36½"
  - 2 strips, 1½" x 14½"

From the gold batik, cut:
- 20 rectangles, 2½" x 4⅜"
- 8 rectangles, 2¼" x 4"

From the cream fabric, cut:
- 40 squares, 2½" x 2½"
- 16 squares, 2¼" x 2¼"
- 4 rectangles, 2¼" x 2½"

Creating the Center Panel

❶ Randomly arrange the cream and tan 3½" squares into 12 rows of four squares each. Sew the squares in each row together. Press the seam allowances in alternate directions from row to row. Sew the rows together. Press the seam allowances in one direction.

❷ Refer to "Fusible-Web Appliqué" (page 8) and use the patterns (page 27) to prepare the individual appliqué pieces from the fabrics indicated. Preassemble the appliqué units using the prepared pieces (see "Preassembling Appliqué Units" on page 9).

❸ Refer to the photo (page 24) to arrange the prepared appliqué units on the background, positioning the pears on the vertical center seam line and about 1" from each end. Follow the manufacturer's instructions to fuse the units in place.

❹ Finish the raw edges of each appliqué piece using a machine blanket stitch, zigzag stitch, or satin stitch.

❺ Square up the center panel to 12½" x 36½".

Assembling the Table-Runner Top

❶ Refer to the table-runner assembly diagram (page 26) to sew the gold metallic-on-black 1½" x 36½" inner-border strips to the sides of the center panel. Press the seam allowances toward the inner-border strips. Sew the gold-metallic-on-black 1½" x 14½" strips to the top and bottom of the center panel. Press the seam allowances toward the inner-border strips.

❷ To make the flying-geese units for the outer border, draw a diagonal line from corner to corner on the wrong side of each cream 2½" square and each cream 2¼" square. Keep the two sizes separated.

❸ Position a marked 2½" square on one end of each gold 2½" x 4⅜" rectangle, right sides together. Sew on the marked lines. Trim ¼" away from the stitching. Press the seam allowances toward the gold rectangles. Repeat on the opposite end of each rectangle, orienting the marked line as shown. These are the flying-geese units for the side borders.

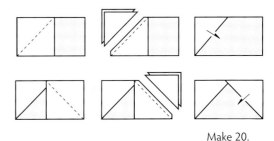

Make 20.

④ Repeat step 3 using the marked cream 2¼" squares and the gold 2¼" x 4" rectangles to make eight flying-geese units. These are the units for the top and bottom borders.

⑤ Sew 10 side-border flying-geese units together side by side, joining them into pairs first. Make sure all the gold points are facing in the same direction. Repeat to make a total of two outer-border strips. Press the seam allowances in one direction. Sew the strips to the sides of the center panel. Press the seam allowances toward the inner-border strips.

⑥ Sew four top/bottom flying-geese units together side by side as described in step 5. Repeat to make a total of two outer-border strips. Add a cream 2¼" x 2½" rectangle to both ends of each strip. Sew these border strips to the top and bottom of the table runner. Press the seam allowances toward the inner-border strips.

Finishing the Table Runner

❶ Trim the backing fabric so that it's 4" longer and 4" wider than the runner top.

❷ Layer the backing, batting, and runner top; baste together.

❸ Quilt as desired.

❹ When the quilting is complete, square up the table-runner sandwich. Refer to "Binding" (page 12) to attach the binding using the gold-metallic-on-black 2½"-wide strips.

❺ Add a label to the back of the table runner.

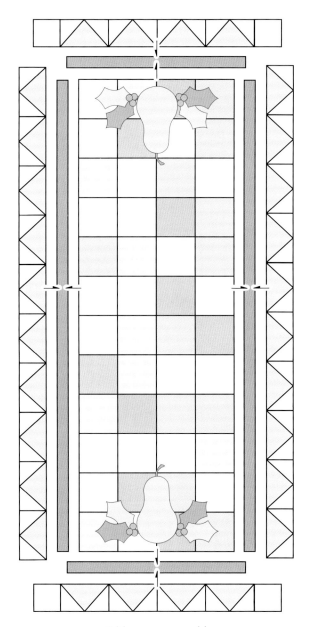

Table-runner assembly

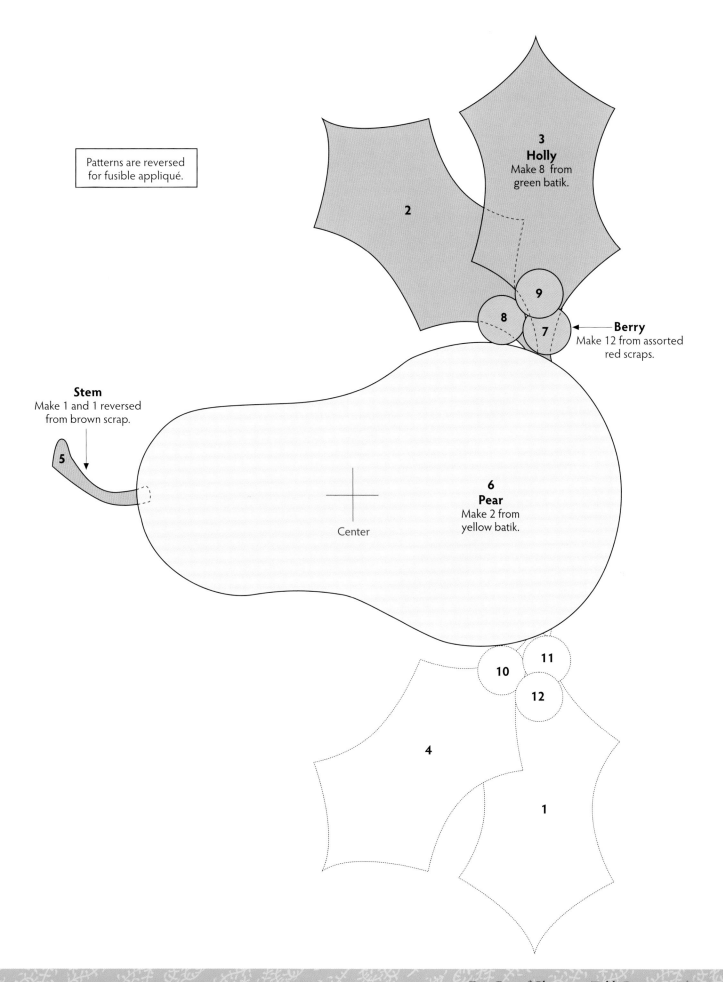

Patterns are reversed
for fusible appliqué.

**3
Holly**
Make 8 from
green batik.

2

9

8

7

Berry
Make 12 from assorted
red scraps.

Stem
Make 1 and 1 reversed
from brown scrap.

5

Center

**6
Pear**
Make 2 from
yellow batik.

10

11

12

4

1

Home for Christmas Bed Runner

Finished bed runner: 85½" x 24½" • *Pieced and appliquéd by Cheryl Almgren Taylor. Quilted by Cheryl Winslow.*

Create this lovely bed runner and "go home" for Christmas, even if you can't travel the miles to get there. Featuring a little red schoolhouse, the local post office, the village church, and a variety of homes, this bed runner evokes the feel of a simpler time and an Americana Christmas.

Materials

Yardage is based on 42"-wide fabric.

1⅛ yards of dark-blue batik for center-panel background

⅞ yard of green batik for inner border, outer-border corner blocks, and binding

7½" x 10" rectangle *each* of tan, light-blue, green, red, white, rust, gold, beige, and sky-blue fabrics for building appliqués

½ yard of red-and-gold metallic plaid for outer border

¼ yard of white tone-on-tone print for center-panel background

Scraps of light-brown, dark-brown, assorted green, black, brick red, bright-red, burgundy, assorted gray, and white fabrics for appliqués

2½ yards of fabric for backing

29" x 90" piece of batting

2 yards of 17"-wide lightweight paper-backed fusible web

Assorted threads to match appliqué fabrics

Gold metallic thread for quilting

Teflon pressing sheet (recommended)

Black ultra-fine-point permanent marker

Cutting

From the dark-blue batik, cut:
- 2 rectangles, 18" x 40"

From the white tone-on-tone print, cut:
- 2 rectangles, 2½" x 40"

From the green batik, cut:
- 6 strips, 2½" x 42"
- 5 strips, 1" x 42"
- 4 squares, 3" x 3"

From the red-and-gold metallic plaid, cut:
- 5 strips, 3" x 42"

Creating the Center Panel

❶ Sew the short sides of the dark-blue 18" x 40" rectangles together to make an 18" x 79½" piece. Press the seam allowances open. Sew the short sides of the white 2½" x 40" rectangles together to make a 2½" x 79½" piece. Press the seam allowances open.

❷ Sew the white piece from step 1 to the blue piece from step 1 along the long edges. Press the seam allowances toward the blue piece.

❸ Refer to "Fusible-Web Appliqué" (page 8) and use the patterns (pages 20, 21, and 31–37) to prepare the individual appliqué pieces. The building numbers on the patterns refer to the order in which they appear on the finished piece, starting on the far left

with building 1. The building main-structure pieces are used for multiple buildings, with the windows, doors, and decorative pieces changing to make each one unique. Consult the materials list and the photo (page 28) for fabric choices as needed. Make the building pieces as follows:

Building 1: Make one each of pieces 1–14 as given on the buildings 1 and 8 pattern.

Building 2: Make piece 4 of the buildings 2, 4, and 7 pattern, following the building 2 roof line. Make the remaining pieces as instructed on the pattern.

Building 3: Make pieces 1 and 2 of the buildings 3, 6, and 9 pattern, following the buildings 3 and 9 roof line for the roof piece. Make the remaining pieces as instructed on the pattern.

Building 4: Make one each of pieces 1–12 as given on the building 2, 4, and 7 pattern, following the building 4 roof line. Use the marker to write the lettering on piece 9.

Building 5: Use the patterns (pages 20 and 21) to make the pieces, eliminating the cross at the top of the steeple, if desired, and substituting the door pattern (page 36).

Building 6: Make one each of pieces 1–10 as given on the building 3, 6, and 9 pattern, following the building 6 roof line. Use the marker to write the lettering on piece 7.

Building 7: Make piece 4 of the buildings 2, 4, and 7 pattern, following the building 2 roof line. Make the remaining pieces as instructed on the pattern.

Building 8: Make pieces 2, 13, and 14 of the buildings 1 and 8 pattern. Make the remaining pieces as instructed on the pattern.

Building 9: Make pieces 1 and 2 of the buildings 3, 6, and 9 pattern, following the buildings 3 and 9 roof line for the roof piece. Make the remaining pieces as instructed on the pattern.

YOUR TOWN, YOUR WAY

This is a great project to customize to your personal needs and taste. Reduce the number of houses and buildings and the size of the center background to create a bed runner for a double or twin bed. Customize the building colors to match your home or neighborhood. Change houses into businesses for a more urban look. Add extra wreaths and garlands for a very festive town. Make it your own special Christmas village.

④ Preassemble the individual buildings and trees using the prepared appliqué pieces (see "Preassembling Appliqué Units" on page 9). Because the pieces are used for several different buildings, the placement order numbers only apply to buildings 1, 4, and 6. For all other buildings, refer to the order number given for individual doors, windows, etc., to assemble those pieces, and then work from the bottom up to assemble your buildings.

⑤ Center building 5 (church) on the center of the background piece from step 2, aligning the bottom of the building with the top of the white strip. Position the remaining buildings and trees, leaving at least ½" of space on the sides for trimming and seam allowances. When you're pleased with the placement, follow the manufacturer's instructions to fuse the pieces in place.

⑥ Finish the raw edges of each piece using a blanket stitch, zigzag stitch, or satin stitch. Use a satin stitch to create the flame for each candle, the center lines on the building 5 (church) and building 6 (post office) doors, and the window panes on building 9.

⑦ Trim the center panel to 79" x 18½".

Assembling the Bed-Runner Top

① Refer to "Adding Borders" (page 11) to add the green 1"-wide inner-border strips to the bed-runner top. Press the seam allowances toward the inner-border strips.

② Measure the length and width of the bed-runner top through the center and make a note of the measurements. From the red-and-gold metallic plaid 3"-wide strips, cut two strips to the length measured for the outer-border side strips and two strips to the width measured for the outer-border top and bottom strips, piecing the strips as needed to achieve the required length. Sew the side borders to the sides of the bed-runner top. Press the seam allowances toward the outer-border strips. Add a green 3" square to both ends of the top and bottom outer-border strips. Press the seam allowances toward the red-and-gold metallic plaid strips. Join these strips to the top and bottom of the bed runner. Press the seam allowances toward the outer-border strips.

Finishing the Bed Runner

① Prepare the backing so that it's 4" longer and 4" wider than the bed-runner top.

② Layer the backing, batting, and bed-runner top; baste together.

③ Quilt as desired.

④ When the quilting is complete, square up the bed-runner sandwich. Refer to "Binding" (page 12) to attach the binding using the green 2½"-wide strips.

⑤ Add a label to the back of the bed runner.

Bed-runner assembly

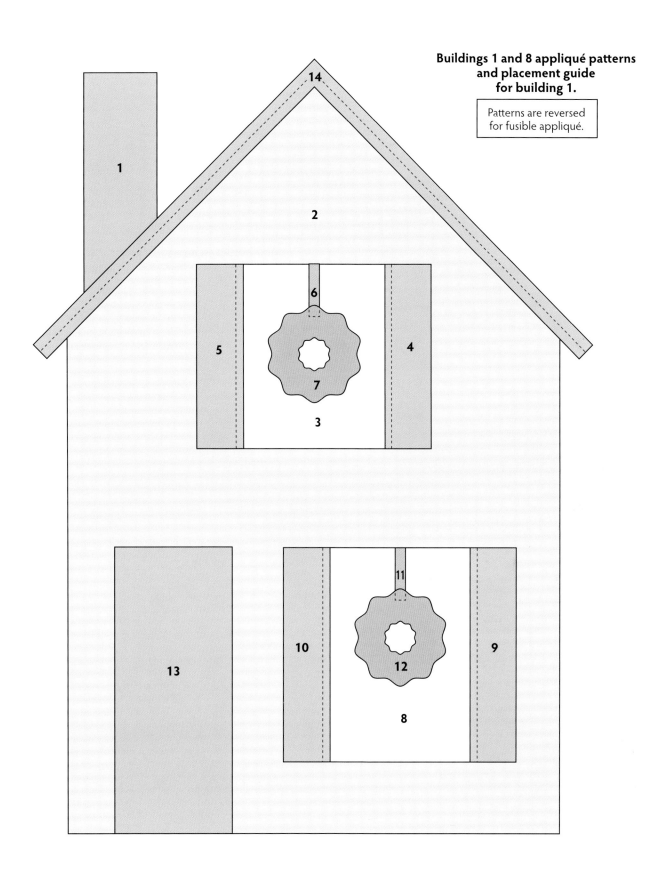

Buildings 1 and 8 appliqué patterns and placement guide for building 1.

Patterns are reversed for fusible appliqué.

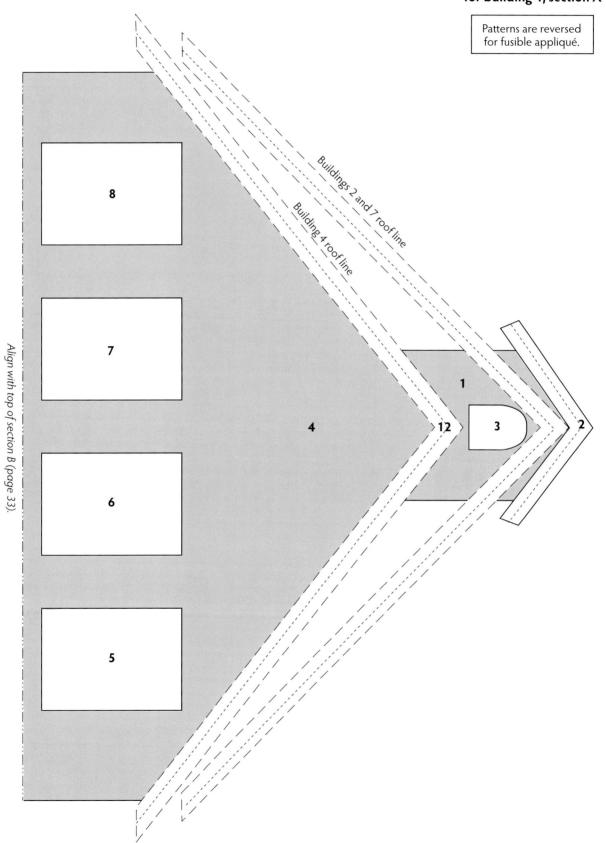

Buildings 2, 4, and 7 appliqué patterns and placement guide for building 4, section A

Patterns are reversed for fusible appliqué.

Buildings 2 and 7 roof line

Building 4 roof line

Align with top of section B (page 33).

8

7

6

5

4

1

12

3

2

**Buildings 2, 4, and 7 appliqué
patterns and placement guide for
building 4, section B**

Patterns are reversed
for fusible appliqué.

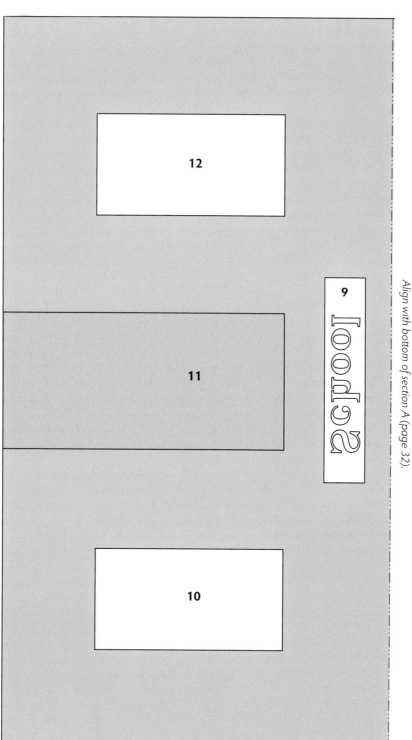

Align with bottom of section A (page 32).

School
9

12

11

10

Patterns are reversed for fusible appliqué.

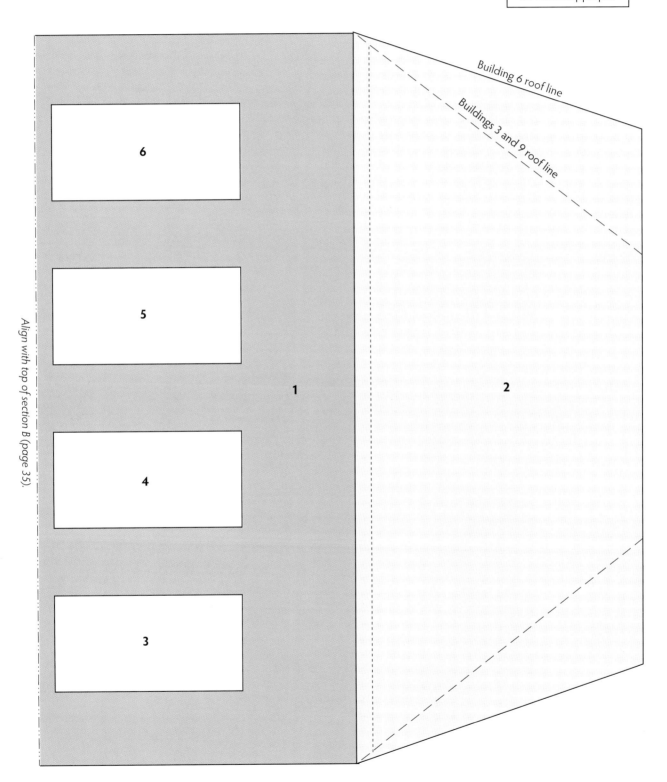

Building 6 roof line

Buildings 3 and 9 roof line

Align with top of section B (page 35).

6

5

1

4

2

3

Section B

Patterns are reversed
for fusible appliqué.

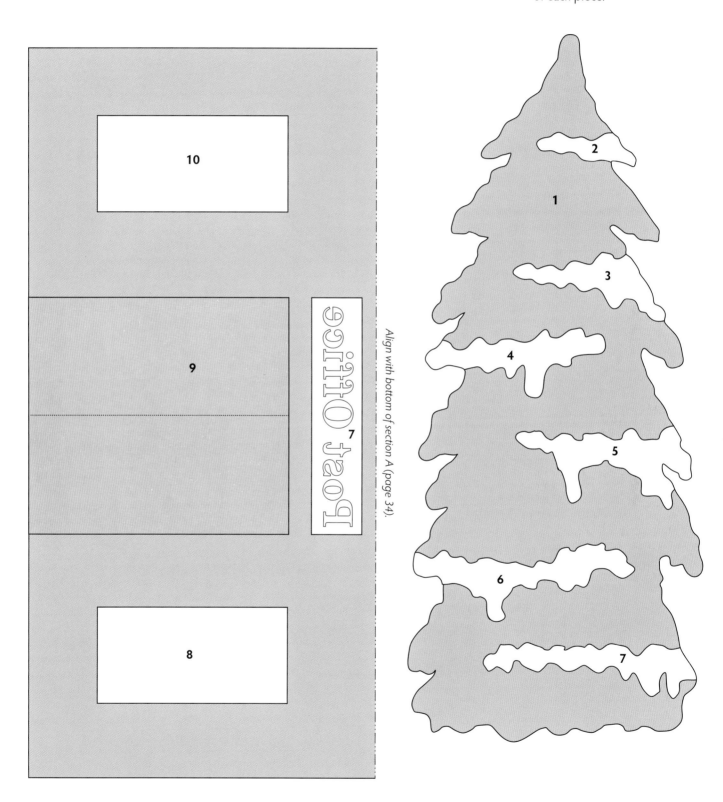

Tree
Make 2 and 2 reversed
of each piece.

10

9

Post Office

7

Align with bottom of section A (page 34).

8

1

2

3

4

5

6

7

Buildings 2 and 7 appliqué patterns

Patterns are reversed
for fusible appliqué.

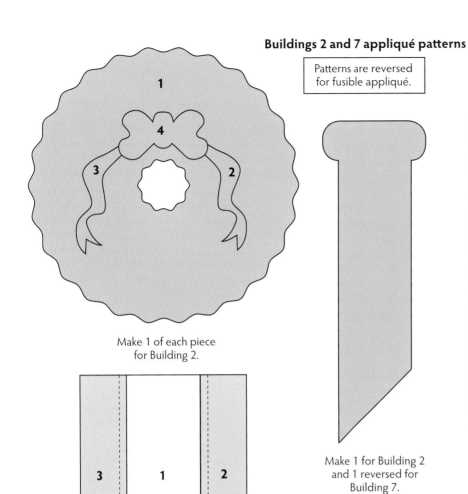

Make 1 of each piece
for Building 2.

Make 1 for Building 2
and 1 reversed for
Building 7.

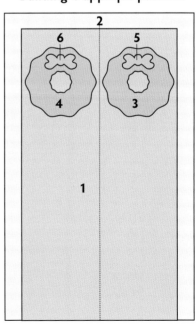

Make 1 door without wreath
for Building 2 and 1 door
with wreath for Building 7.

Make 5 of each piece
for Buildings 2 and 7.

Building 8 appliqué patterns

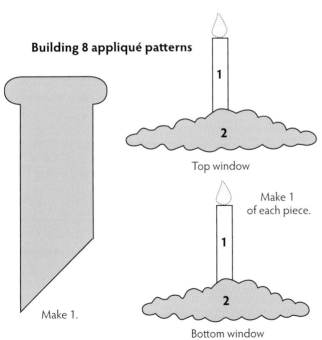

Top window

Make 1
of each piece.

Make 1.

Bottom window

Building 5 appliqué patterns

Make 1 of each piece.

Building 9 appliqué patterns

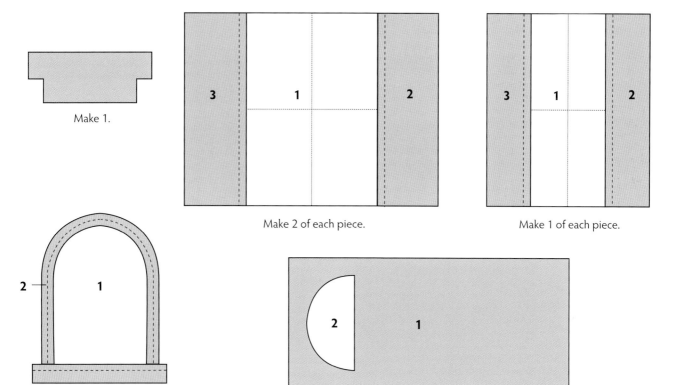

Make 1.

Make 2 of each piece.

Make 1 of each piece.

Make 1 of each piece.

Make 1 of each piece.

Building 3 appliqué patterns

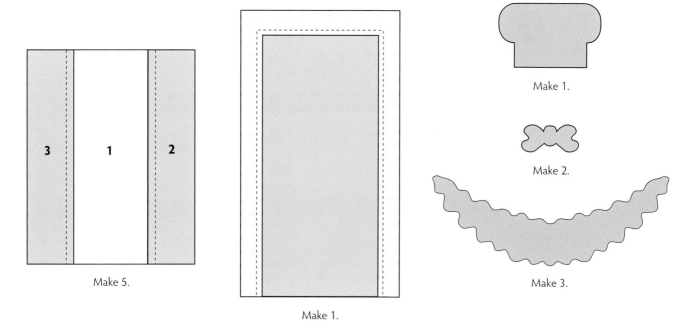

Make 5.

Make 1.

Make 1.

Make 2.

Make 3.

Christmas Greetings Card Holder

Finished card holder: 26½" x 31" • *Pieced and quilted by Cheryl Almgren Taylor.*

*This Christmas wall hanging is festive yet functional as it holds
and displays beautiful holiday cards. A touch of appliqué and
easy straight stitching make it a quick project and a great gift.*

Materials

Yardage is based on 42"-wide fabric.

¾ yard of medium-red holly print for pocket interiors and flaps

¾ yard of dark-red print for berry appliqués, narrow sashing, inner border, and binding

½ yard of green pine-needle print for pocket interiors and flaps

⅜ yard of green print for holly appliqués and outer border

⅜ yard of white candy-cane print for pocket exteriors

¼ yard of dark-red holly print for pocket exteriors

¼ yard of light-green plaid for wide sashing

1 yard of fabric for backing

31" x 35" piece of batting

1 yard of 20"-wide lightweight fusible interfacing

1 yard of 17"-wide lightweight paper-backed fusible web

Assorted threads to match appliqué fabrics

Teflon pressing sheet (recommended)

Cutting

From the light-green plaid, cut:
- 3 strips, 2½" x 20½"

From *each* of the fusible interfacing and paper-backed fusible web, cut:
- 6 rectangles, 6½" x 8¾"
- 2 rectangles, 9¾" x 10⅛"

From the medium-red holly print, cut:
- 2 rectangles, 9¾" x 10⅛"
- 2 strips, 6½" x 42"; crosscut into:
    - 2 rectangles, 6½" x 9¾"
    - 3 rectangles, 6½" x 8¾"
    - 3 rectangles, 6½" x 5½"

From the green pine-needle print, cut:
- 3 rectangles, 6½" x 8¾"
- 3 rectangles, 5½" x 6½"

From the white candy-cane print, cut:
- 2 rectangles, 6⅛" x 9¾"
- 3 rectangles, 5¼" x 6½"

From the dark-red holly print, cut:
- 3 rectangles, 5¼" x 6½"

From the dark-red print, cut:
- 4 strips, 2½" x 42"
- 4 strips, 1½" x 42". From *each* strip, cut 1 rectangle, 1½" x 5½" (4 total). Set aside the remainder of the strips for the inner borders.
- 1 rectangle, 2" x 6½"
- 5 strips, 1" x 20½"

From the green print, cut:
- 4 strips, 2½" x 42"

Preparing the Appliquéd Sashing

❶ Refer to "Fusible-Web Appliqué" (page 8) and use the patterns (page 41) to prepare the individual appliqué pieces from the fabrics indicated. Preassemble the holly units using the prepared appliqué pieces (see "Preassembling Appliqué Units" on page 9).

CONFUSABLE FUSIBLES

Two types of fusible products are being used in this project. Fusible *web* is used to adhere the holly and berry appliqué to the background fabric. Fusible *interfacing* is used to strengthen the card pockets. Be careful not to mix up the products or you'll have problems!

❷ Fold one of the light-green plaid strips in half lengthwise and crosswise, then finger-press the creases to mark the center. Refer to the photo (page 38) to evenly space the prepared appliqué units on the strip, beginning at the center and working outward. Follow the manufacturer's instructions to fuse the pieces in place, leaving at least ½" of space on each side for trimming and seam allowances.

❸ Finish the raw edges of each appliqué piece with a machine blanket stitch, zigzag stitch, or satin stitch.

Assembling the Envelope Pockets

❶ Follow the manufacturer's instructions to fuse the *interfacing* 6½" x 8¾" rectangles to the wrong sides of the medium-red holly print and green pine-needle print 6½" x 8¾" rectangles. Repeat with the interfacing and medium-red holly print 9¾" x 10⅛" rectangles.

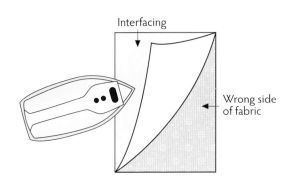

Interfacing

Wrong side of fabric

❷ Follow the manufacturer's instructions to fuse the corresponding-sized paper-backed fusible web rectangle to the interfaced side of each of the rectangles from step 1.

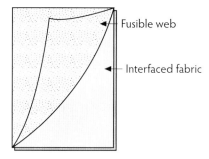

Fusible web

Interfaced fabric

DO THE TWO-STEP

Most of the double-sided fusible interfacing products available are heavyweight, making them extremely stiff, and fairly pricey. Although this two-step process seems redundant, I think it works better than the double-sided interfacings. I don't recommend heavyweight products for this project.

❸ Use a pencil or fabric marker to mark the center of one short edge of the fused rectangles. Make another mark along both sides of each rectangle the distance indicated. Draw a line from each side mark to the bottom center mark to form a V. Cut along the marked lines.

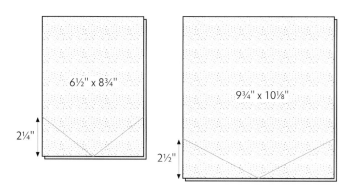

6½" x 8¾"

2¼"

9¾" x 10⅛"

2½"

❹ Peel away the backing paper. On the fusible side of each medium-red holly print 6½" x 8¾" rectangle, place a candy-cane print 5¼" x 6½" rectangle *right* side up (wrong sides together) at the straight end. The medium-red holly fabric will extend beyond the candy cane fabric. Repeat for the medium-red holly print 9¾" x 10⅛" rectangles and the candy-cane print 6⅛" x 9¾" rectangles. Follow the manufacturer's

instructions to fuse the rectangles in place, being careful not to let the iron touch the exposed fusible web on the V-shaped end.

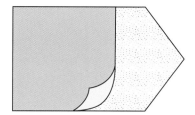

❺ Repeat step 4 with the green pine-needle print 6½" x 8¾" rectangles and the dark-red holly print 5¼" x 6½" rectangles.

❻ Carefully fold the V-shaped end of each unit over the adhered rectangle, making sure the fold is exactly at the end of the smaller piece of fabric. This will create a flap for the front of the envelope pockets. Fuse the V-shaped flap to the front of the fabric.

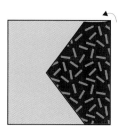

❼ Using a machine blanket stitch, satin stitch, or zigzag stitch, finish the raw edges on each of the envelope flaps.

❽ With right sides up, pair each of the small envelope units with a 5½" x 6½" backing rectangle of fabric that matches the flap, aligning the bottom of the envelopes with the backing rectangle. The backing rectangle will extend ¼" above the top of the envelope flap. In the same manner, pair each of the large envelope units with a medium-red holly print 6½" x 9¾" rectangle. Baste the sides of the units together, making sure there are no folds or tucks.

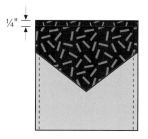

¼"

Baste.

Assembling the Card-Holder Top

❶ Arrange the small envelopes and dark-red 1½" x 5½" sashing rectangles into two rows as shown. Arrange the large envelopes and dark-red 2" x 6½" sashing rectangle into a row as shown. Sew the pieces in each row together. Press the seam allowances toward the sashing rectangles.

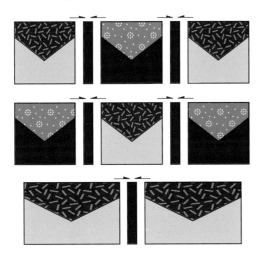

❷ Refer to the card-holder assembly diagram at right to arrange the light-green plaid 2½" x 20½" sashing strips, the dark-red 1" x 20½" sashing strips, and the envelope rows as shown. Sew the strips and rows together, making sure that only the backing section of the envelope rows is sewn into the seams, not the top of the envelopes. Press the seam allowances as indicated.

❸ Refer to "Adding Borders" (page 11) to measure the card-holder top for the borders. Add the dark-red 1½"-wide inner-border strips to the card-holder

top first, and then add the green 2½"-wide outer-border strips.

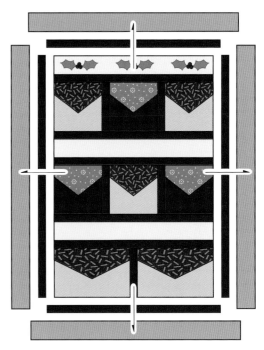

Card-holder assembly

Finishing the Card Holder

❶ Prepare the backing so that it's 4" longer and 4" wider than the card-holder top.

❷ Layer the backing, batting, and card-holder top; baste together.

❸ Quilt the sashings, borders, and areas around the envelope pockets. Do not quilt the pockets themselves.

❹ When the quilting is complete, trim the card-holder sandwich. Refer to "Binding" (page 12) to attach the binding using the dark-red 2½"-wide strips.

❺ Add a hanging sleeve and a label to the back of the card holder.

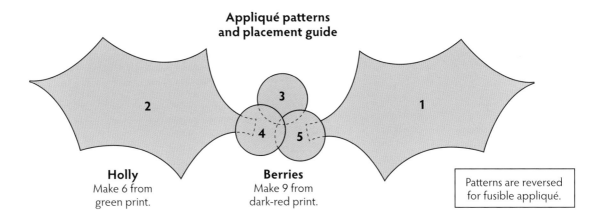

Appliqué patterns and placement guide

2

3

4   5

1

Holly
Make 6 from green print.

Berries
Make 9 from dark-red print.

Patterns are reversed for fusible appliqué.

Christmas Pageant Wall Hanging

Finished wall hanging: 22½" x 14" ● *Pieced and quilted by Cheryl Almgren Taylor.*

This small wall hanging brings back memories of holiday plays at school and Christmas pageants at church. Fun to complete as a weekend project with very little piecing, it's a cheerful addition to any holiday decor.

Materials

Yardage is based on 42"-wide fabric.

⅜ yard of tan batik for background

⅜ yard of black fabric for inner border and binding

¼ yard of red print for outer border

Scraps of assorted medium-green, dark-green, tan, black, brown, yellow, red, light-blue, royal-blue, orange, white, and purple prints for appliqués

½ yard of fabric for backing

27" x 18" piece of batting

½ yard of 17"-wide lightweight paper-backed fusible web

Black thread

Assorted threads to match appliqué fabrics

Black ultra-fine-point permanent marker

Teflon pressing sheet (recommended)

Cutting

From the tan batik, cut:
- 1 rectangle, 9½" x 18"

From the black fabric, cut:
- 2 strips, 1" x 42"
- 3 strips, 2½" x 42"

From the red print, cut:
- 3 strips, 2½" x 42"

Creating the Center Panel

❶ Refer to "Fusible-Web Appliqué" (page 8) and use the patterns (pages 44 and 45) to prepare the individual appliqué pieces. Consult the materials list and the photo (page 42) for fabric choices as needed. Preassemble the appliqué units for each child using the prepared pieces (see "Preassembling Appliqué Units" on page 9). Use the marker to add the eyes, eyeglasses, and clothing details as indicated on the pattern.

❷ Arrange the prepared appliqué units and letter appliqués on the tan rectangle. Refer to the manufacturer's instructions to fuse the pieces in place, leaving at least ½" of space on each side for trimming and seam allowances.

❸ Trace the banner line onto the center panel. Machine stitch over the drawn line using black thread and a narrow satin stitch to create the banner string.

❹ Finish the raw edges of each appliqué piece using a machine blanket stitch, zigzag stitch, or satin stitch.

❺ Trim the center panel to 17½" x 9".

Adding Borders

Refer to "Adding Borders" (page 11) to measure the wall-hanging top for the borders. Add the black 1"-wide inner-border strips to the wall-hanging top first, and then add the red print 2½"-wide outer-border strips to the quilt top.

Finishing the Wall Hanging

❶ Prepare the backing so that it's 4" longer and 4" wider than the wall hanging-top.

❷ Layer the backing, batting, and wall-hanging top; baste together.

❸ Quilt as desired.

❹ When the quilting is complete, square up the wall-hanging sandwich. Refer to "Binding" (page 12) to attach the binding using the black 2½"-wide strips.

❺ Add a hanging sleeve and a label to the back of the wall hanging.

Wall-hanging assembly

Banner
stitching
line

**Appliqué patterns
and placement guide, section B**

Patterns are reversed
for fusible appliqué.

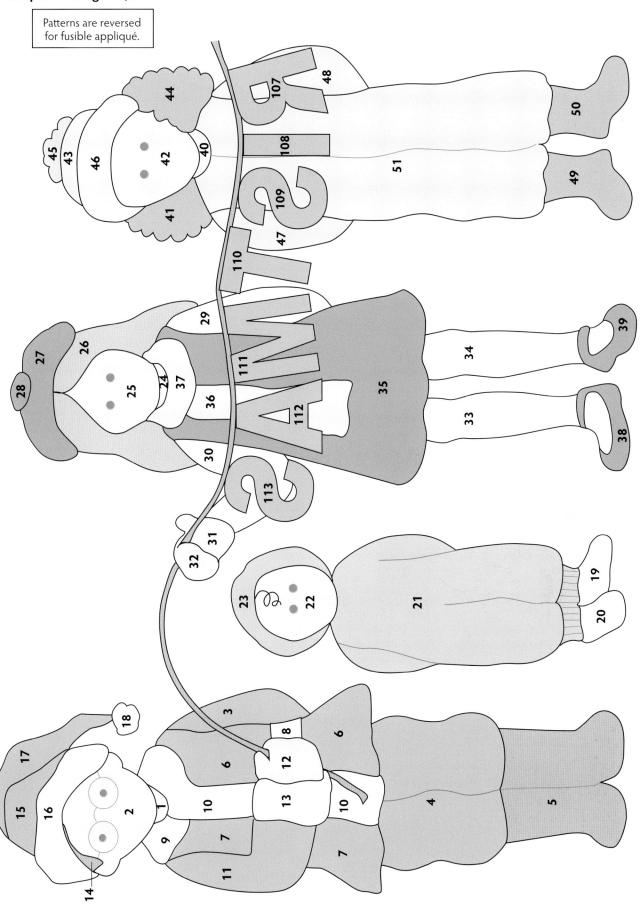

Celebrate the Season

Most families have traditions at Christmastime that make their celebration more meaningful, and it isn't unusual for there to be a display of cherished items that are only seen during this season. What better occasion to create a special quilted treasure that becomes a part of your family's annual festivities? Create the stunning "Christmas Bouquet Wall Hanging" (page 48) so that it will sparkle in your home every Christmas, or the "Night Before Christmas Quilt" (page 56) to snuggle in as you read Clement Clarke Moore's poem to your little ones. If you don't have time for an extended project, pick one of the fast and festive table runners to set the stage for holiday dining. Quilts can make any celebration more meaningful.

Christmas Bouquet Wall Hanging

Finished wall hanging: 36½" x 36½" • *Pieced and appliquéd by Cheryl Almgren Taylor. Quilted by Cheryl Winslow.*

Though it may be snowy and cold outside, Christmas flowers bloom in your home with this lovely appliquéd quilt. Metallic threads and sparkling embellishments add a touch of glitter to the Christmas season and brighten your Christmas celebration.

Materials

Yardage is based on 42"-wide fabric.

1¼ yards of red batik for setting triangles, pieced outer border, and binding

1 yard of white tone-on-tone print #1 for center blocks and pieced outer border

⅝ yard of medium-green batik for poinsettia leaf appliqués, center-block unit frame, and inner border

1 fat quarter *each* of 4 assorted red-and-gold metallic prints for center-block appliqués

1 fat quarter of pine-green batik for holly-leaf appliqués

1 fat quarter of white tone-on-tone print #2 for setting-triangle poinsettia appliqués

1 fat eighth of gold metallic print for berry appliqués

1⅓ yards of fabric for backing

40" x 40" piece of batting

1 yard of 17"-wide lightweight paper-backed fusible web

120 gold hot-fix crystals or metallic beads for poinsettia centers and setting-triangle vines

Assorted threads to match appliqué fabrics

Gold metallic thread for appliqué

Metallic needle (recommended)

Teflon pressing sheet (recommended)

Cutting

From white tone-on-tone print #1, cut:
- 4 squares, 9" x 9"
- 32 squares, 4½" x 4½"

From the medium-green batik, cut:
- 2 strips, 1¾" x 19"
- 2 strips, 1¾" x 16½"
- 2 strips, 1½" x 28½"
- 2 strips, 1½" x 26½"

From the red batik, cut:
- 2 squares, 14" x 14"; cut in half diagonally to yield 4 triangles
- 9 strips, 2½" x 42"; crosscut 5 *of the strips* into 68 squares, 2½" x 2½"

Appliquéing the Center-Block Units

1. Refer to "Fusible-Web Appliqué" (page 8) and use the patterns (pages 52–55) to prepare the individual appliqué pieces from the fabrics indicated. You might want to plan ahead and decide which two red-and-gold metallic fabrics you'll use for each of the red poinsettias. Preassemble the poinsettia units using the prepared pieces (see "Preassembling Appliqué Units" on page 9).

2. For the center blocks, center a prepared red poinsettia appliqué unit on each white 9" square. Follow the manufacturer's instructions to fuse the units in place.

3. For the setting triangles, arrange a prepared white poinsettia and holly-vine appliqué unit on each red triangle. Allow at least ½" of space on all sides for trimming and seam allowances. Follow the manufacturer's instructions to fuse the pieces in place.

4. Finish the raw edges of each appliqué piece using a machine blanket stitch, zigzag stitch, or satin stitch.

5. Square up the center blocks to 8½" x 8½". Do not trim the setting triangles at this point.

Assembling the Wall-Hanging Top

1. Arrange the red poinsettia center blocks into two rows of two blocks each. Sew the blocks in each row together. Press the seam allowances in opposite directions. Sew the rows together. Press the seam allowances in one direction.

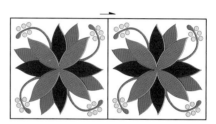

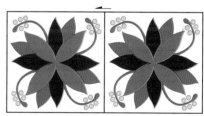

② Sew the medium-green 1¾" x 16½" strips to opposite sides of the center-block unit. Press the seam allowances toward the strips. Add the medium-green 1¾" x 19" strips to the top and bottom of the unit. Press the seam allowances toward the strips.

❸ Fold each appliquéd setting triangle right sides together along the long edge and finger-press the fold to mark the center. With the center points matching the seams of the center-block unit, sew an appliquéd setting triangle to opposite sides of the unit. The triangles are slightly larger than necessary and will be trimmed when the center-block unit is complete. Press the seam allowances toward the medium-green strips. Repeat on the opposite sides of the center unit with the remaining setting triangles. Square up the center-block unit to measure 26½" x 26½".

Adding the Borders

❶ Refer to the wall-hanging assembly diagram to sew the medium-green 1½" x 26½" inner-border strips to the sides of the center-block unit. Press the seam allowances toward the strips. Sew the medium-green 1½" x 28½" inner-border strips to the top and bottom of the center-block unit. Press the seam allowances toward the strips. The wall-hanging top must measure 28½" x 28½" in order for the pieced border to fit.

BORDER PATROL

If your top doesn't measure 28½" x 28½" at this point, adjustments can be made. If it's too small, use a narrower seam allowance to attach the inner-border strips, or if you have enough fabric, cut wider strips. If the top is too large, carefully trim an equal amount from each side or use a wider seam allowance to attach the inner-border strips.

② To make the pieced border, draw a diagonal line from corner to corner on the wrong side of each red 2½" square.

❸ Place a marked square on the upper-left corner of a white 4½" square, right sides together. Sew on the line. Trim ¼" away from the stitching. Press the seam allowances toward the red fabric. Place another red square on the upper-right corner of the 4½" square, orienting the line as shown. Sew, trim, and press as before. Repeat to make a total of 32 units.

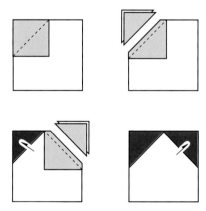

Make 32.

④ Place a remaining marked square on the lower-right corner of a unit from step 3, orienting the marked line as shown. Sew, trim, and press as before. Make four units for the corners.

Make 4.

⑤ Sew eight units from step 3 together side by side as shown. The strip should measure 28½". Repeat to make a total of four strips.

Make 4.

⑥ Refer to the wall-hanging assembly diagram below to sew strips from step 5 to the sides of the wall-hanging top. Press the seam allowances toward the inner border. Add a unit from step 4 to each end of the remaining two strips. Press the seam allowances toward the units from step 5. Add these strips to the top and bottom of the wall-hanging top. Press the seam allowances toward the inner border.

Finishing the Wall Hanging

① Prepare the backing so that it's 4" longer and 4" wider than the wall-hanging top.

② Layer the backing, batting, and wall-hanging top; baste together.

③ Quilt as desired.

④ When the quilting is complete, square up the wall-hanging sandwich. Refer to "Binding" (page 12) to attach the binding using the red 2½"-wide strips.

⑤ Attach hot-fix crystals or beads using your preferred method. I used hot-fix crystals (heat transference method), but some embellishments use glue or can be hand sewn to the quilt top.

⑥ Add a hanging sleeve and a label to the back of your wall hanging.

Wall-hanging assembly

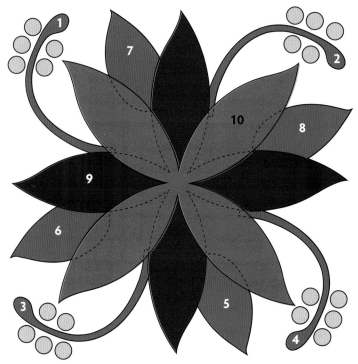

Placement guide

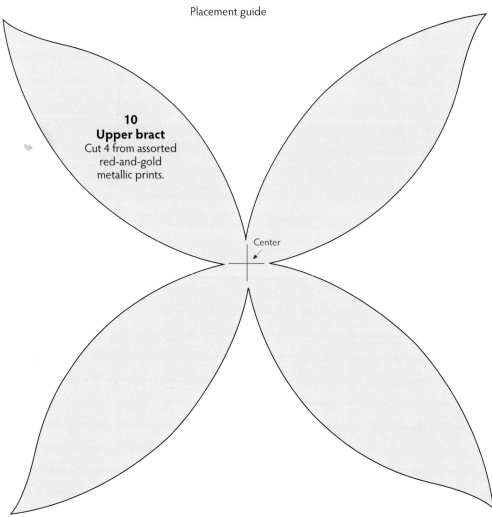

10
Upper bract
Cut 4 from assorted red-and-gold metallic prints.

Center

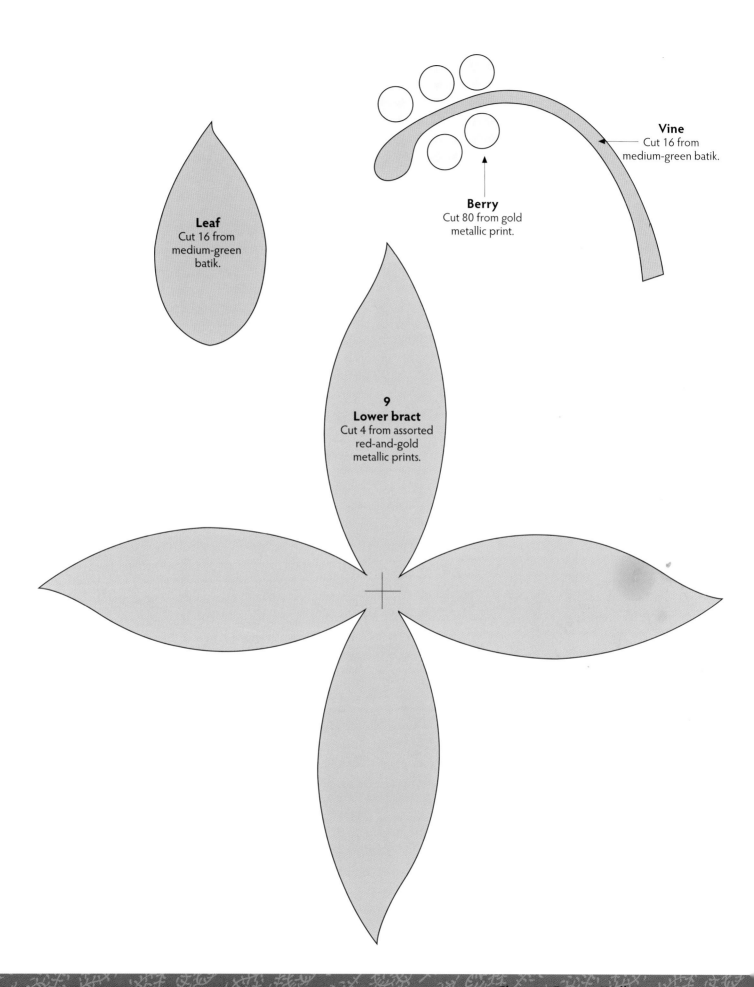

Leaf
Cut 16 from
medium-green
batik.

Vine
Cut 16 from
medium-green batik.

Berry
Cut 80 from gold
metallic print.

9
Lower bract
Cut 4 from assorted
red-and-gold
metallic prints.

Patterns are reversed
for fusible appliqué.

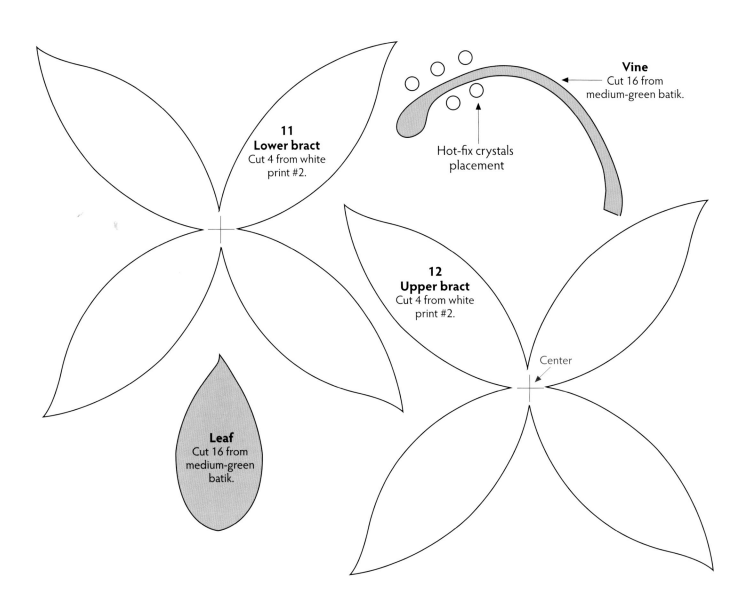

11

9

12

3

4

10

Align with
left side holly-vine
pattern (page 55).

8

7

5

6

Align with right side
holly-vine pattern (page 55).

Placement guide

**11
Lower bract**
Cut 4 from white
print #2.

Vine
Cut 16 from
medium-green batik.

Hot-fix crystals
placement

**12
Upper bract**
Cut 4 from white
print #2.

Center

Leaf
Cut 16 from
medium-green
batik.

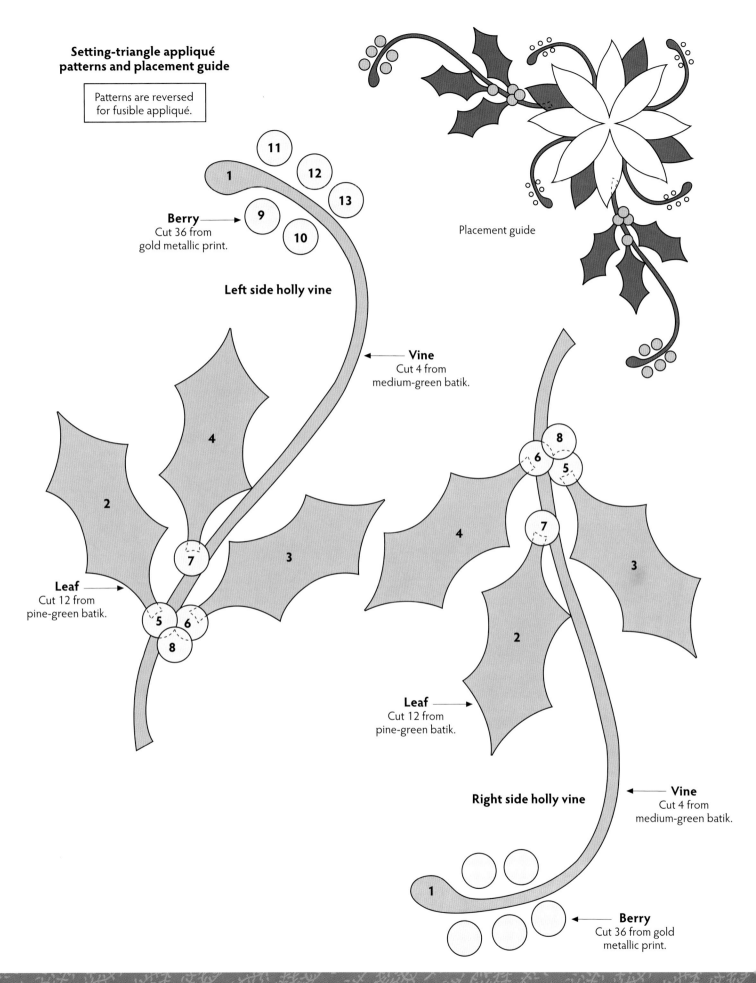

Setting-triangle appliqué patterns and placement guide

Patterns are reversed for fusible appliqué.

11

1

12

13

Berry
Cut 36 from gold metallic print.

9

10

Left side holly vine

Vine
Cut 4 from medium-green batik.

Placement guide

4

2

3

7

Leaf
Cut 12 from pine-green batik.

5

6

8

8

6

5

7

4

3

2

Leaf
Cut 12 from pine-green batik.

Right side holly vine

Vine
Cut 4 from medium-green batik.

1

Berry
Cut 36 from gold metallic print.

Night Before Christmas Quilt

Finished quilt: 49½" x 49½" • *Pieced and appliquéd by Cheryl Almgren Taylor. Quilted by Cheryl Winslow.*

The stockings are hung and the packages wait beneath the tree in this quilted tribute to Clement Clarke Moore's cherished Christmas poem. Simple appliqué shapes and easy piecing make this quilt a breeze, though it appears complex and time consuming. Enjoy the compliments it's sure to bring!

Materials

Yardage is based on 42"-wide fabric.

1 fat quarter *each* of green-checked fabric, cream holly print, red holly print, green mottled print, red-checked fabric, red plaid, and red mottled print for appliqués

1⅝ yards of red batik for bow appliqués, sashing, inner border, pieced outer border, and binding

1⅛ yards of light-green batik for stocking, ornament, and package rows and outer-border corner blocks

¾ yard of white tone-on-tone print for pieced outer border

⅝ yard of apple-green print for background of Christmas lights rows

7" x 11" rectangle *each* of bright-green batik, green batik, and red print for bow appliqués

Scraps of assorted blue, black, yellow, orange, red, and gold metallic batiks and holiday prints for lights, ornament, and stocking appliqués

3 yards of fabric for backing

54" x 54" piece of batting

1 yard of 17"-wide lightweight paper-backed fusible web

1⅓ yards of ¼"-wide gold metallic fusible bias tape

Assorted threads to match appliqué fabrics

50-weight black thread

Gold metallic thread for appliqué

Metallic needle (recommended)

Teflon pressing sheet (recommended)

Stabilizer or tissue paper (optional)

Cutting

From the light-green batik, cut:
- 4 strips, 9" x 42"; crosscut into:
  - 5 rectangles, 9" x 10"
  - 5 squares, 9" x 9"
  - 3 rectangles, 9" x 4"
  - 2 rectangles, 9" x 3"
- 4 squares, 4" x 4"

From *each* of the red batik, red plaid, and green batik, cut:
- 1 rectangle, 1½" x 6"

From *each* of the red print and bright-green batik rectangles, cut:*
- 1 rectangle, 1½" x 7"

From *each* of the red mottled, cream holly, and green mottled print fat quarters, cut:*
- 2 rectangles, 4½" x 6"

From *each* of the green-checked and red holly print fat quarters, cut:*
- 2 rectangles, 4½" x 7"

From the apple-green print, cut:
- 2 strips, 6" x 41" (If your fabric isn't wide enough, cut 3 strips, piece them together end to end, and then cut two strips to the required length.)

From the white tone-on-tone print, cut:
- 24 rectangles, 4" x 7½"

From the red batik, cut:*
- 6 strips, 2½" x 42"
- 3 strips, 2" x 42"
- 4 strips, 1½" x 40½"
- 2 strips, 1½" x 39½"
- 48 squares, 4" x 4"

Reserve the remainder of these fabrics for appliqué pieces.

Preparing the Appliqués

Refer to "Fusible-Web Appliqué" (page 8) and the patterns (pages 60–65) to prepare the individual appliqué pieces for the quilt. Preassemble the stockings, Christmas lights, ornaments, and bows using the prepared pieces (see "Preassembling Appliqué Units" on page 9).

Assembling the Block Rows

❶ To make the Stocking blocks, center a prepared stocking unit on each light-green 9" x 10" rectangle, leaving at least ½" of space on each side for trimming and seam allowances. Follow the manufacturer's instructions to fuse the units in place.

❷ To make the Ornament blocks, cut five strips, 4¾" long, and five strips, 3¼" long, from the gold metallic fusible bias tape. Referring to the photo (page 56) as needed, arrange one 4¾"-long strip and one 3¼"-long strip on each light-green 9" square, placing the longer strip on the left of the block and the shorter strip on the right of the block. One end of each strip should be aligned with the top edge of the square. Position a prepared large ornament unit at the end of the longer strip and a prepared small ornament unit at the end of the shorter strip. Allow at least ½" of space on each side for trimming and seam allowances. Follow the manufacturer's instructions to fuse the units in place.

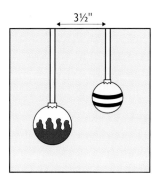

③ To make the Package blocks, select a three-loop bow and matching 1½" x 6" rectangle for each small package and a two-loop bow and matching 1½" x 7" rectangle for each large package.

④ Sew matching 4½" x 6" rectangles to opposite sides of a 1½" x 6" rectangle. Press the seam allowances toward the center rectangle. Add a light-green 9" x 4" rectangle to the top of this unit. Press the seam allowances toward the light-green rectangle. Repeat to make a total of three small package units. In the same manner, sew matching 4½" x 7" rectangles to opposite sides of a 1½" x 7" rectangle; press. Add a light-green 9" x 3" rectangle to the top of this unit; press. Repeat to make a total of two large package units.

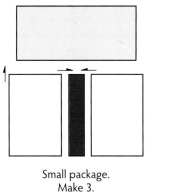 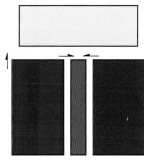

Small package.
Make 3.

Large package.
Make 2.

⑤ Position a prepared bow that matches each ribbon on the green rectangle, centering the bow on the ribbon. Follow the manufacturer's instructions to fuse the bow units in place.

Small Package block.
Make 3.

Large Package block.
Make 2.

⑥ Finish the raw edges of each stocking, ornament, and bow appliqué piece using a machine blanket stitch, zigzag stitch, or satin stitch.

⑦ Trim the Stocking blocks to 8½" x 9½". Trim the Ornament blocks and Package blocks to 8½" x 8½" (it's ok to trim the bias tape at the top of the Ornament blocks).

⑧ Referring to the photo (page 56) as needed, sew the Stocking blocks together side by side along their long edges. Press the seam allowances in one direction. Sew the Ornament blocks together in the same manner. Press the seam allowances in one direction. Alternately sew the small and large Package blocks together side by side. Press the seam allowances in one direction.

Appliquéing the Christmas Lights Rows

① Referring to the photo and using a pencil or fabric marker, draw a curving, loopy line on *each* of the two apple-green 6" x 41" strips. Make the line different on each of the strips.

② Using a satin stitch and 50-weight black thread, stitch over the drawn line to create the electrical string for the Christmas lights. You may need to go over the stitching twice to create a solid line.

3 Position the prepared Christmas light units along the electrical string of each strip. You will have 11 lights on one strip and 12 lights on the other strip. Follow the manufacturer's instructions to fuse the units in place.

4 Finish the raw edges of each appliqué piece using a machine blanket stitch, zigzag stitch, or satin stitch.

5 Trim the rows to 5½" x 40½", leaving at least ½" of space on each side.

6 Sew a red 1½" x 40½" sashing strip to the top and bottom of each row. Press the seam allowances toward the red strips.

Assembling the Quilt Top

1 Refer to the quilt assembly diagram (page 60) to sew the block rows and Christmas lights rows together. Press the seam allowances toward the Christmas lights rows.

2 Sew the red 1½" x 39½" inner-border strips to the sides of the quilt top. Press the seam allowances toward the inner-border strips. Sew the red 2" x 42" inner-border strips together end to end to make one long strip. From the pieced strip, cut two strips, 2" x 42½". Sew these strips to the top and bottom of the quilt top. Press the seam allowances toward the inner-border strips. The quilt top must measure 42½" x 42½" in order for the pieced border to fit. If it doesn't, refer to "Border Patrol" (page 50) for ways to make adjustments.

3 To make the flying-geese units for the pieced border, draw a diagonal line from corner to corner on the wrong side of each red 4" square.

4 Place a marked square on one end of each white 4" x 7½" rectangle, right sides together. Sew on the marked line. Trim ¼" from the stitching. Press the seam allowances toward the red fabric. Repeat on the opposite end of each rectangle, orienting the marked line as shown.

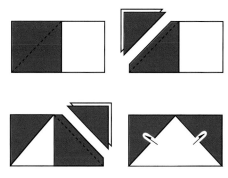

Make 24.

5 Sew six flying-geese units together side by side, joining them into pairs first. Make sure all the points are facing the same direction. Repeat to make a total of four rows. Press the seam allowances in one direction.

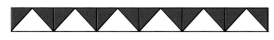

Make 4.

6 Refer to the quilt assembly diagram to sew pieced outer-border strips to the sides of the quilt top. Press the seam allowances toward the outer border. To each end of the remaining two pieced border strips, sew a light-green 4" square. Press the seam allowances toward the pieced border. Sew these borders to the top and bottom of the quilt top. Press the seam allowances toward the outer border.

Finishing the Quilt

1 Prepare the backing so that it's 4" longer and 4" wider than the quilt top.

2 Layer the backing, batting, and quilt top; baste together.

3 Quilt as desired.

4 When the quilting is complete, square up the quilt sandwich. Refer to "Binding" (page 12) to attach the binding using the red 2½"-wide strips.

5 Add a hanging sleeve and a label to the back of the quilt.

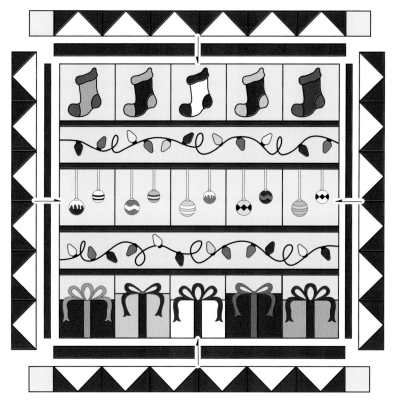

Quilt assembly

Placement guide

Christmas light appliqué patterns and placement guide

2
Bulb
Cut 23 from
assorted scraps.

1

Base
Cut 23 from black.

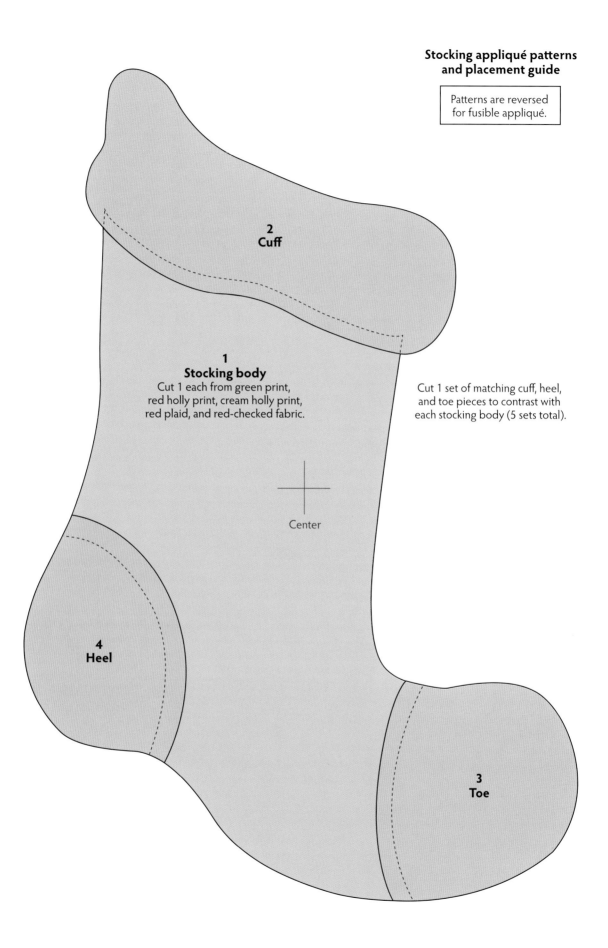

Patterns are reversed
for fusible appliqué.

**2
Cuff**

**1
Stocking body**
Cut 1 each from green print,
red holly print, cream holly print,
red plaid, and red-checked fabric.

Cut 1 set of matching cuff, heel,
and toe pieces to contrast with
each stocking body (5 sets total).

Center

**4
Heel**

**3
Toe**

**Large ornament appliqué patterns
and placement guides**

Patterns are reversed
for fusible appliqué.

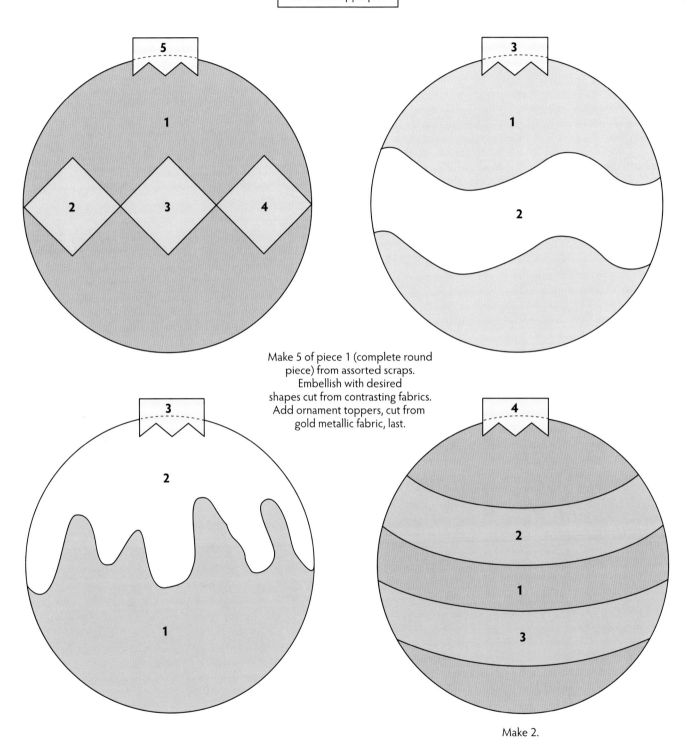

Make 5 of piece 1 (complete round
piece) from assorted scraps.
Embellish with desired
shapes cut from contrasting fabrics.
Add ornament toppers, cut from
gold metallic fabric, last.

Make 2.

Small ornament appliqué patterns and placement guides

Patterns are reversed for fusible appliqué.

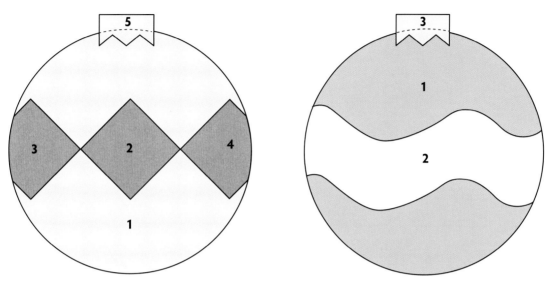

Make 5 of piece 1 (complete round piece) from assorted scraps. Embellish with desired shapes cut from contrasting fabrics. Add ornament toppers, cut from gold metallic fabric, last.

Using a striped fabric for pieces 2 and 3 enables you to cut one strip for the middle.

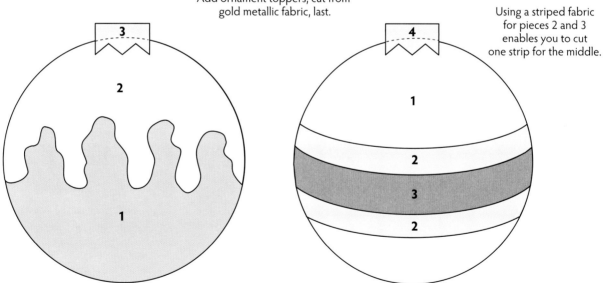

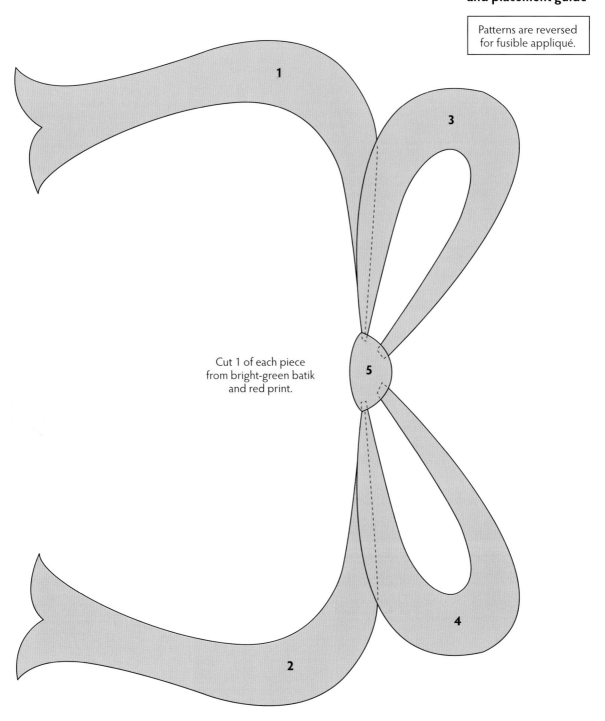

2-loop bow appliqué patterns and placement guide

Patterns are reversed for fusible appliqué.

Cut 1 of each piece from bright-green batik and red print.

1

3

5

2

4

Patterns are reversed
for fusible appliqué.

1

3

5

Cut 1 of each piece
from red batik,
red plaid, and green batik.

4

2

Christmas Ornaments Table Runner

Finished table runner: 12½" x 48½" • *Pieced and appliquéd by Cheryl Almgren Taylor. Quilted by Cheryl Winslow.*

Add some glitz to your Christmas dining with this table runner featuring metallic fabrics that sparkle by candlelight. Ornaments hang from purchased gold metallic fusible bias tape, and the entire project can be completed in a day.

Materials

Yardage is based on 42"-wide fabric.

⅔ yard of green-and-gold metallic print for background

½ yard of red print for center block and binding

¼ yard of cream-and-gold metallic print for center block and ornament appliqués

⅛ yard of red batik for ornament appliqués

⅞ yard of fabric for backing

16" x 53" piece of batting

1⅞ yards of ¼"-wide gold metallic fusible bias tape

½ yard of 17"-wide lightweight paper-backed fusible web

Assorted threads to match appliqué fabrics

Gold metallic thread for appliqué

Metallic needle (recommended)

Cutting

From the cream-and-gold metallic print, cut:
- 1 square, 5" x 5"

From the red print, cut:
- 5 strips, 2½" x 42"; crosscut *1 of the strips,* into:
    2 rectangles, 2½" x 9"
    2 rectangles, 2½" x 5"

From the green-and-gold metallic print, cut:
- 1 strip, 12½" x 42"; crosscut into 2 squares, 12½" x 12½"
- 1 square, 9⅜" x 9⅜"; cut in half diagonally to yield 2 triangles
- 2 squares, 6⅞" x 6⅞"; cut in half diagonally to yield 4 triangles

Assembling the Table-Runner Background

① Sew red 2½" x 5" rectangles to the sides of the cream-and-gold metallic 5" square. Press the seam allowances toward the rectangles. Sew red 2½" x 9" rectangles to the top and bottom of the square. Press the seam allowances toward the rectangles.

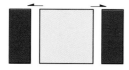

② Sew green-and-gold metallic 6⅞" triangles to opposite sides of the center square from step 1. Press the seam allowances toward the triangles. Repeat on the remaining two sides of the center square. Square up the block to 12½" x 12½".

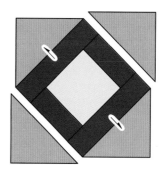

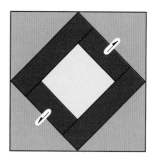

③ Join the green-and-gold metallic 12½" squares to the sides of the center block from step 2. Press the seam allowances toward the squares. Sew a green-and-gold metallic 9⅜" triangle to each end of the joined squares. Press the seam allowances toward the triangles.

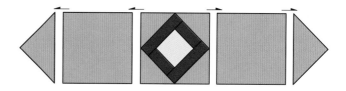

Appliquéing the Table-Runner Top

① From the gold metallic fusible bias tape, cut two 12" lengths and four 8½" lengths. Mark a 12"-long line on each side of the center block that begins at the outer point of the center block and is parallel to the long sides of the table runner. On each side of these lines, mark two more lines that are 2½" from the edge of the table runner's long sides and extend 8½" from the center block. Fuse the bias tape lengths to these lines.

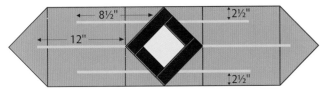

Table-runner assembly

❷ Refer to "Fusible-Web Appliqué" (page 8) and use the patterns below to prepare the individual appliqué pieces. Preassemble the ornaments using the prepared pieces (see "Preassembling Appliqué Units" on page 9).

❸ Follow the manufacturer's instructions to fuse the prepared ornament appliqué units in place.

❹ Finish the raw edges of each appliqué piece using a machine blanket stitch, zigzag stitch, or satin stitch.

Finishing the Table Runner

❶ Trim the backing fabric so that it's 4" longer and 4" wider than the table-runner top.

❷ Layer the backing, batting, and table-runner top; baste together.

❸ Quilt as desired.

❹ When the quilting is done, square up the table-runner sandwich. Refer to "Binding Odd Angles" (page 13) to attach the binding using the remaining red 2½"-wide strips.

❺ Add a label to the back of the table runner.

EASY PEASY APPLIQUÉ

To finish your table runner even faster, cut your ornaments from a piece of fabric printed with ornament motifs. All you need to do is apply fusible web to the wrong side of the fabric, cut out the shapes, and fuse them in place!

Ornament appliqué patterns and placement guide

> Patterns are reversed for fusible appliqué.

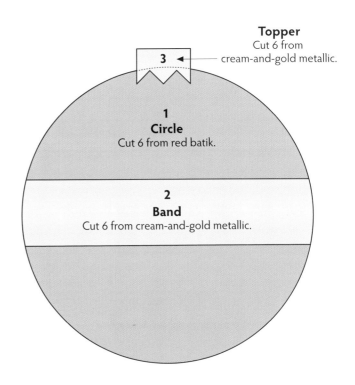

Topper
Cut 6 from cream-and-gold metallic.

3

1
Circle
Cut 6 from red batik.

2
Band
Cut 6 from cream-and-gold metallic.

Holly Jolly Christmas Quilt

Finished quilt: 45½" x 56¾" • *Pieced and appliquéd by Cheryl Almgren Taylor. Quilted by Cheryl Winslow.*

This versatile quilt is perfect as a lap quilt to snuggle under, a table covering to brighten your decor, or a wall quilt to bring season's greetings to your room. With basic piecing and large appliqué pieces that are easy enough for a beginner, it's fast and simple to create. The use of two shades of both green and red in the appliqué adds interest to the design.

Materials

Yardage is based on 42"-wide fabric.

1½ yards of white tone-on-tone print for appliqué block backgrounds and outer-border berry appliqués

1 yard of red plaid for pieced blocks, pieced setting triangles, and outer border

1 yard of green batik #1 for holly appliqués, inner border, and binding

½ yard of apple-green print for pieced blocks and pieced setting triangles

⅜ yard of red batik for berry appliqués, pieced blocks, pieced setting triangles, and outer-border corner blocks

¼ yard of green batik #2 for holly appliqués

Scrap of red fabric for berry appliqués

2⅞ yards of fabric for backing

50" x 61" piece of batting

1 yard of 17"-wide lightweight paper-backed fusible web

Assorted threads to match appliqué fabrics

Teflon pressing sheet (recommended)

Cutting

From the white tone-on-tone print, cut:
- 1 square, 12⅝" x 12⅝"; cut into quarters diagonally to yield 4 triangles
- 16 squares, 9" x 9"

From the apple-green print, cut:
- 1 strip, 9¾" x 42"; crosscut:
    - 2 squares, 9¾" x 9¾"; cut into quarters diagonally to yield 8 side setting triangles (you'll have 2 left over)
    - 2 squares, 6½" x 6½"
- 2 squares, 5⅛" x 5⅛"; cut in half diagonally to yield 4 corner setting triangles

From the red plaid, cut:
- 5 strips, 5" x 42"
- 24 rectangles, 1½" x 6½"

From the red batik, cut:
- 4 squares, 5½" x 5½"
- 34 squares, 1½" x 1½"

From green batik #1, cut:
- 6 strips, 2½" x 42"
- 5 strips, 1½" x 42"

Making the Appliquéd Pieces

❶ Refer to "Fusible-Web Appliqué" (page 8) and use the patterns (pages 73 and 74) to prepare the individual appliqué pieces. Preassemble the large and medium holly units, pairing the green #1 leaves with the red batik berries and the green #2 leaves with the red scrap berries (see "Preassembling Appliqué Units on page 9). Preassemble the border holly units, using a mixture of green leaves for each unit.

❷ Position a large holly unit on one corner of each white 9" square using the placement lines. Position a medium holly unit on each white triangle using the placement lines. Center a border holly unit on each red batik 5½" square, leaving at least ½" on each side for trimming and seam allowances. Follow the manufacturer's instructions to fuse the units in place.

> ### FOLLOW THE LINES
> It's important to follow the placement lines when positioning the holly units on the white squares and rectangles so there will be a consistent amount of space around them and so that the appliqués won't be caught in the seam allowances.

❸ Finish the raw edges of each appliqué piece using a machine blanket stitch, zigzag stitch, or satin stitch.

❹ Trim the white 9" blocks to 8½" x 8½", leaving a ¼" seam allowance around the berries. Square up the red 5½" outer-border blocks to 5" x 5", keeping the appliqué unit centered. Do not trim the white setting triangles.

Making the Pieced Blocks and Setting Triangles

❶ To make the pieced blocks, sew a red batik 1½" square on one end of a red plaid 1½" x 6½" rectangle. Make 20 units. Press the seam allowances toward the rectangles. Set aside six of these units and label them unit A. To the remaining 14 units, sew a red

1½" square to the opposite end of the 6½" rectangle. Press the seam allowances toward the rectangles. Label these unit B.

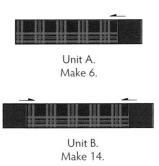

Unit A.
Make 6.

Unit B.
Make 14.

❷ Sew red plaid 1½" x 6½" rectangles to opposite sides of each apple-green 6½" square. Press the seam allowances toward the rectangles. Add a B unit to the top and bottom of each square. Press the seam allowances toward the B units.

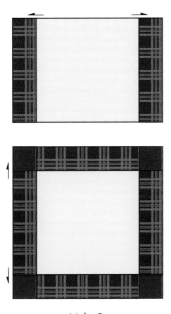

Make 2.

❸ To make the pieced side setting triangles, sew an A unit to the short side of each apple-green side setting triangle as shown, making sure the end of the plaid rectangle lines up with the bottom of the triangle. The red square on the end of the A unit will extend past the triangle. Press the seam allowances toward the A units. On the adjacent short side of each triangle, sew a B unit, aligning the red square on the B

unit with the plaid rectangle of the A unit. Press the seam allowances toward the B units.

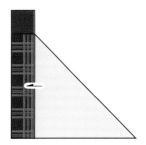

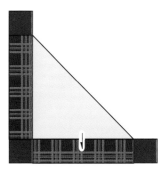

Make 6.

❹ Trim the A and B units even with the long diagonal edge of the apple-green triangle, making sure the ¼" line of the ruler is aligned with the diagonal center of the red squares.

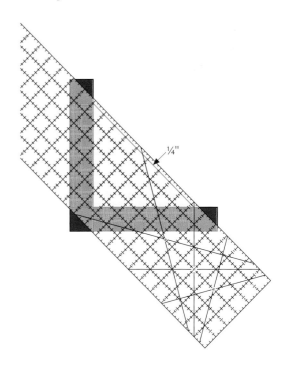

¼"

5 To make the pieced corner setting triangles, fold each apple-green corner setting triangle in half along the long edge and crease the fold to find the center. Fold the remaining B units in half crosswise and crease the fold. With the crease marks matching, sew a B unit to the long side of each triangle. Press the seam allowances toward the B units. Trim the B units even with the short sides of the triangle, making sure the ¼" line of the ruler is aligned with the diagonal center of the red squares.

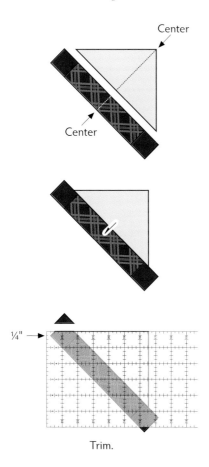

Center

Center

¼" →

Trim.

Assembling the Quilt Top

1 Refer to the quilt assembly diagram (page 73) to arrange the blocks and setting triangles into diagonal rows. Sew the blocks and side setting triangles into rows. Press the seam allowances in alternating directions from row to row. Sew the rows together, adding the corner triangles to the quilt top last. Press the seam allowances away from the center row. The white appliquéd side setting triangles were cut slightly oversized; trim them even with the sides of the quilt top if necessary, being careful to leave ¼" of seam allowance from the point of the holly leaves. Square up the corners of the quilt top as well.

2 Refer to "Adding Borders" (page 11) to add the 1½"-wide green #1 inner-border strips to the quilt top, piecing the strips as necessary. Press the seam allowances toward the border strips.

3 Measure the length and width of the quilt top through the center and make a note of the measurements. From the red plaid 5"-wide strips, cut two strips to the length measured for the outer-border side strips and two strips to the width measured for the outer-border top and bottom strips, piecing the strips as needed to achieve the required length. Sew the side borders to the sides of the quilt top. Press the seam allowances toward the outer-border strips. Add an outer-border appliquéd holly block to each end of the outer-border top and bottom strips. Press the seam allowances toward the plaid strips. Join these strips to the top and bottom of the quilt top. Press the seam allowances toward the outer-border strips.

Finishing the Quilt

1 Prepare the backing so that it's 4" longer and 4" wider than the quilt top.

2 Layer the backing, batting, and quilt top; baste together.

3 Quilt as desired.

4 When the quilting is complete, square up the quilt sandwich. Refer to "Binding" (page 12) to attach the binding using the 2½"-wide green #1 strips.

5 If you'll be using your quilt as a wall hanging, add a hanging sleeve. Also, add a label to the back of the quilt.

Quilt assembly

**Outer-border holly appliqué patterns
and placement guide**

Inner leaf
Cut 2 from
green batik #1
and 2 from
green batik #2.

3

1

Outer leaf
Cut 4 from
green batik #1
and 4 from
green batik #2.

5

4

Berry
Cut 12 from
white tone-on-tone
print.

2

6

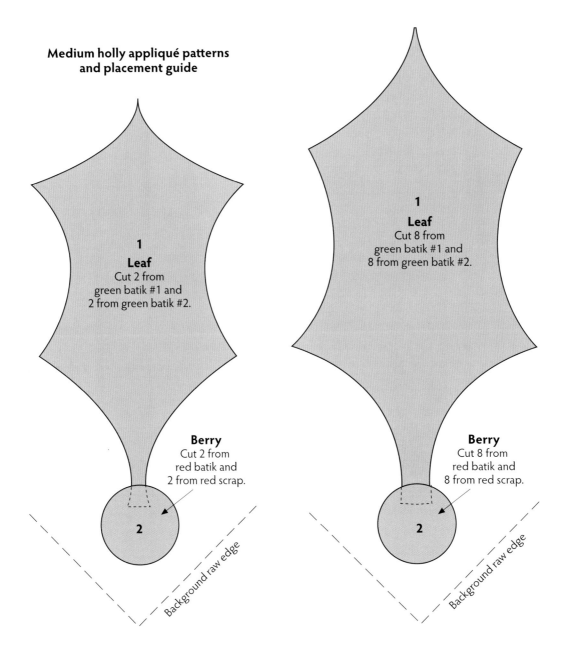

Large holly appliqué patterns and placement guide

Medium holly appliqué patterns and placement guide

1

Leaf
Cut 2 from
green batik #1 and
2 from green batik #2.

1

Leaf
Cut 8 from
green batik #1 and
8 from green batik #2.

Berry
Cut 2 from
red batik and
2 from red scrap.

Berry
Cut 8 from
red batik and
8 from red scrap.

2

2

Background raw edge

Background raw edge

Candy Canes Table Runner

Finished table runner: 15" x 43" ● *Pieced and quilted by Cheryl Almgren Taylor.*

*This whimsical table runner is fast and easy to make. Scrappy prairie
points finish the edges and bright-red fabrics create a visual pop.
It's perfect to set the mood for a Christmas celebration.*

Materials

Yardage is based on 42"-wide fabric.

½ yard *total* of assorted red fabrics for prairie-point border

⅜ yard of white tone-on-tone print for center background

¼ yard of deep-green batik for bow appliqués and inner border

Scraps of white and assorted red fabrics and dark-green batik for candy-cane appliqués

1 yard of fabric for backing

16" x 44" piece of batting

½ yard of 17"-wide lightweight paper-backed fusible web

Assorted threads to match appliqué fabrics

Teflon pressing sheet (recommended)

Cutting

From the white tone-on-tone print, cut:
- 1 rectangle, 11" x 39"

From the deep-green batik, cut:
- 3 strips, 1½" x 42"

From the assorted red fabrics for the prairie-point border, cut a *total* of:
- 52 squares, 3" x 3"

Assembling the Table-Runner Top

1. Refer to "Fusible-Web Appliqué" (page 8) and use the patterns (page 77) to prepare the individual appliqué pieces. Preassemble four candy-cane units from the prepared pieces (see "Preassembling Appliqué Units" on page 9).

2. Refer to the photo (page 75) or the table-runner assembly diagram (page 77) to equally space the candy-cane units on the white rectangle, leaving at least ½" of space at each end. Follow the manufacturer's instructions to fuse the units in place.

3. Finish the raw edges of each appliqué piece using a machine blanket stitch, zigzag stitch, or satin stitch.

4. Trim the center panel to 10½" x 38½".

5. Refer to "Adding Borders" (page 11) to add the deep-green 1½"-wide inner-border strips to the table-runner top. Press the seam allowances toward the border strips.

Finishing the Table Runner

1. Prepare the backing so that it's 4" longer and 4" wider than the table-runner top.

2. Layer the backing, batting, and table-runner top; baste the layers together.

3. Quilt as desired, making sure that your quilting stitches stop at least ½" from the edges of the table-runner top to allow room for attaching the prairie points and turning under the seam allowances.

4. To make the prairie points, fold each red 3" square in half diagonally, wrong sides together; press. Fold the triangles in half again; press.

Make 52.

5. Fold the backing fabric away from the edges of the table-runner top. Randomly arrange 20 prairie points along the long edges of the table-runner top, aligning the base of the triangles with the raw edge of the table-runner top. Slip the fold of one point into the opening of the previous point, making sure the points are evenly spaced; pin in place. In the same manner, arrange six prairie points along each short end. Using a ¼" seam allowance, sew through the table-runner top and batting, sewing the prairie points in place. Do not catch the backing fabric in the seam.

Table runner top

6. Trim the batting close to the stitching. Fold the prairie points out, turning the seam allowance in toward the batting, and lightly press from the right side. Trim the backing fabric so that it extends ⅜" beyond the edges of the table-runner top. Turn the seam allowance of the backing under, covering the seam allowance and the machine stitches of the prairie points. Hand stitch the backing in place.

7. Add a label to the back of the table runner.

Table-runner assembly

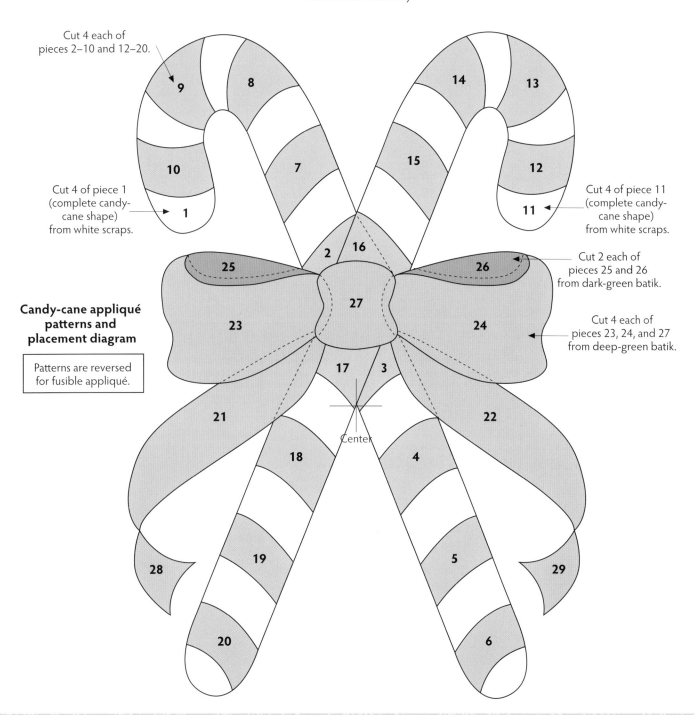

Cut 4 each of pieces 2–10 and 12–20.

9 8 14 13

10 7 15 12

Cut 4 of piece 1 (complete candy-cane shape) from white scraps.

1 11 Cut 4 of piece 11 (complete candy-cane shape) from white scraps.

2 16

25 26 Cut 2 each of pieces 25 and 26 from dark-green batik.

27

Candy-cane appliqué patterns and placement diagram

23 24 Cut 4 each of pieces 23, 24, and 27 from deep-green batik.

Patterns are reversed for fusible appliqué.

17 3

21 22

Center

18 4

28 29

19 5

20 6

Rejoice and Be Glad!

Christmas is a time for joy and laughter and celebrations. But for people of faith, it's a season of reflection and spiritual significance as well. Beyond the fun, beyond the tinsel and presents and food, this is a time to acknowledge the gift of the Christ child and his birth. The "Keeping Watch O'er Their Flocks Pillow" (page 80), "Glad Tidings Table Runner" (page 84), and "Rejoice Wall Hanging" (page 88) are designed to express the reason we celebrate this season. They bring the real story of Christmas into our celebrations. So rejoice and be glad!

Keeping Watch O'er Their Flocks Pillow

Finished pillow: 16" x 16" • *Pieced and appliquéd by Cheryl Almgren Taylor.*

The star of Bethlehem shines down on a shepherd with his sheep on this small Christmas pillow. Simple to make and a lovely gift, it tells the story of the first Christmas night.

Materials

Yardage is based on 42"-wide fabric.

⅝ yard of blue batik for appliqué background and pillow back

¼ yard of light-green batik for appliqué background

¼ yard of deep-green batik for flat piping

⅛ yard of tan batik for border

Scraps of assorted tan, peach, green, brown, black, and gold fabrics for appliqués

¼ yard of 17"-wide lightweight paper-backed fusible web

Assorted threads to match appliqué fabrics

Black ultra-fine-point permanent marker

16" x 16" square pillow form

Teflon pressing sheet (recommended)

Cutting

From the blue batik, cut:
- 1 strip, 16½" x 42"; crosscut into:
    - 2 rectangles, 16½" x 11"
    - 1 rectangle, 15" x 11"

From the light-green batik, cut:
- 1 rectangle, 5" x 15"

From the tan batik, cut:
- 2 rectangles, 1½" x 16½"
- 2 rectangles, 1½" x 14½"

From the deep-green batik, cut:
- Enough ⅞"-wide bias strips to make a 70" length when pieced together

Creating the Pillow Front

❶ Refer to "Fusible-Web Appliqué" (page 8) and use the patterns (page 83) to prepare the individual appliqué pieces. Consult the photo (page 80) and the materials list above for fabric choices as needed. Preassemble the sheep, sheep-and-shepherd, and star units using the prepared pieces (see "Preassembling Appliqué Units" on page 9). Use the marker to make the dots for the shepherd's eyes where indicated on the pattern.

❷ Sew the light-green 5" x 15" rectangle to the blue 15" x 11" rectangle along the 15"-long edges to make the background piece. Press the seam allowances toward the green.

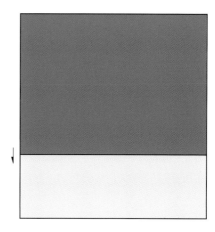

❸ Refer to the photo to arrange the prepared appliqué units on the background piece, leaving at least ½" on all sides for trimming and seam allowances. Follow the manufacturer's instructions to fuse the units in place.

❹ Finish the raw edges of each appliqué piece using a machine blanket stitch, zigzag stitch, or satin stitch.

❺ Square up the pillow top to 14½" x 14½".

❻ Sew the tan 1½" x 14½" strips to the sides of the pillow top. Press the seam allowances towards the tan strips. Sew the tan 1½" x 16½" strips to the top and bottom of the pillow top. Press the seam allowances towards the tan strips.

Pillow assembly

Adding the Piping

❶ Join the deep-green bias strips to make one long strip. To join the strips, place the ends of two strips right sides together, forming an angle that looks like the bottom half of the letter X. Stitch the strips together as shown. Press the seam allowances open and trim to ¼", if needed. Join the remaining strips in the same way.

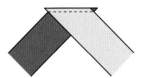

❷ Press the strip in half lengthwise, wrong sides together.

❸ With the raw edges aligned, baste the piping strip to the pillow top edges using a ¼" seam allowance and leaving a 3" tail unstitched at the beginning. Wrap the strip as tightly as possible around the corners.

❹ When you're approximately 2½" from the beginning of the strip, overlap the beginning and end of the strip. Mark a line halfway between the two ends of both overlapped strips. You need to mark both strips in exactly the same spot. Unfold both ends of the strip and place them right sides together. Sew the ends together on the marked line. Trim ¼" away from the stitching.

❺ Refold the piping and finish basting it in place.

Finishing the Pillow

❶ To make the pillow back, fold under and press ¼" of one long edge on each blue 16½" x 11" rectangle. Fold under the pressed edge ¼" again; press. Stitch along the folded edges.

❷ With right sides together and raw edges aligned, place the hemmed rectangles on the pillow top with the hemmed edges overlapping. Turn the layered pieces over so that the pillow top is wrong side up; pin the pieces together. Following the piping stitching line, sew around the pillow.

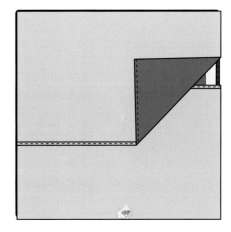

❸ Turn the pillow cover to the right side and insert the pillow form through the opening in the back.

Glad Tidings Table Runner

Finished table runner: 14" x 40" • *Pieced and quilted by Cheryl Almgren Taylor.*

Angels were the first to announce the news of the birth of Jesus on the first Christmas.
Made from whole cloth with no seams or piecing, this beautiful table runner
features angel appliqués that stand out from the turquoise-sky background.
A few metallic prints give the table runner a bit of Christmas sparkle.

Materials

Yardage is based on 42"-wide fabric.

½ yard of turquoise-and-gold metallic print for background

⅜ yard of cream-and-gold metallic print for wing appliqués and binding

1 fat quarter of white tone-on-tone print for angel appliqués

Scraps of peach, cream, honey yellow, and gold fabrics for appliqués

1⅓ yard of fabric for backing

18" x 44" piece of batting

½ yard of 17"-wide lightweight paper-backed fusible web

Assorted threads to match appliqué fabrics

Gold metallic thread for appliqué

Metallic needle (recommended)

Teflon pressing sheet (recommended)

Cutting

From the turquoise-and-gold metallic print, cut:
- 1 rectangle, 14" x 40"

From the cream-and-gold metallic print, cut:
- 3 strips, 2½" x 42"

Creating the Table Runner

1. Refer to "Fusible-Web Appliqué" (page 8) and use the patterns (pages 86 and 87) to prepare the individual appliqué pieces. Consult the photo (page 84) and the materials list above for fabric choices as needed. Preassemble two angel units using the prepared pieces (see "Preassembling Appliqué Units" on page 9).

2. Center a prepared appliqué unit 1½" from each end of the turquoise-and-gold metallic rectangle. Follow the manufacturer's instructions to fuse the units in place.

3. Finish the raw edges of each appliqué piece using a machine blanket stitch, zigzag stitch, or satin stitch.

4. Use a pencil or fabric marker to make a mark 4" from each corner on both sides of the table-runner top. Draw a diagonal line connecting the points. Cut on the lines to angle the corners.

Finishing the Table Runner

1. Prepare the backing so that it's 4" longer and 4" wider than the table-runner top.

2. Layer the backing, batting, and table-runner top; baste together.

3. Quilt as desired.

4. Trim the backing and batting even with the table-runner top. Refer to "Binding Odd Angles" (page 13) to attach the binding using the cream-and-gold metallic 2½"-wide strips.

5. Add a label to the back of the table runner.

**Angel appliqué patterns
and placement guide, section A**

Patterns are reversed
for fusible appliqué.

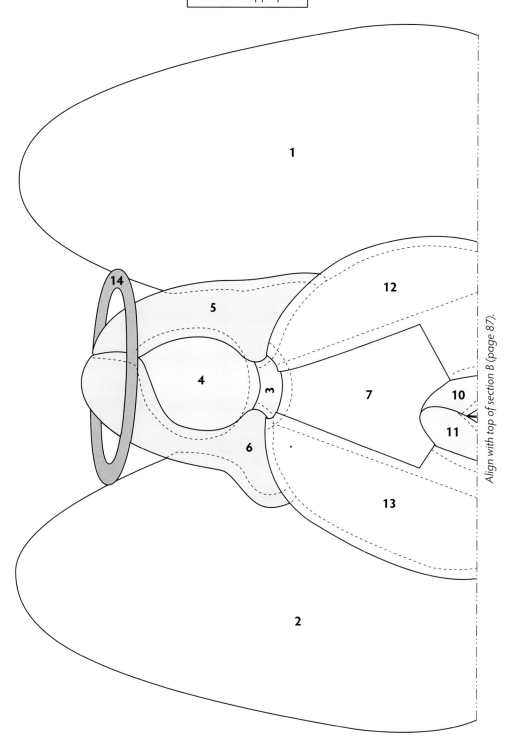

1

14

5

12

4

3

7

10

6

11

13

2

Align with top of section B (page 87).

Angel appliqué patterns
and placement guide, section B

Patterns are reversed
for fusible appliqué.

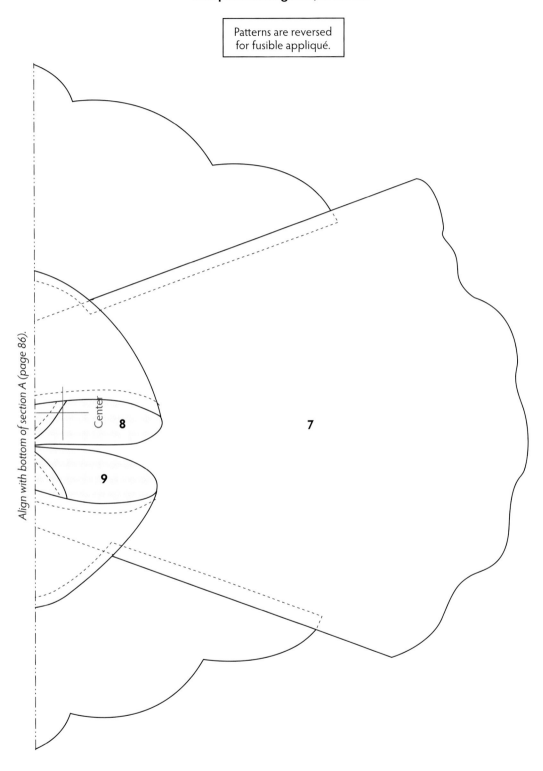

Align with bottom of section A (page 86).

Center

8

9

7

Rejoice Wall Hanging

Finished wall hanging: 18½" x 26¾" • *Pieced and quilted by Cheryl Almgren Taylor.*

*This sweet and simple wall hanging displays the reason
for the season—the birth of the baby Jesus.*

Materials

Yardage is based on 42"-wide fabric.

½ yard of dark-blue batik for manger background

½ yard of tan metallic print for letter background and outer border

⅓ yard of dark-gold metallic print for letters, sashing, inner border, outer-border corner blocks, and binding

1 fat quarter of cream metallic print for star appliqué

Scraps of gold metallic, peach, light-blue, yellow, and brown fabrics for appliqués

⅝ yard of fabric for backing

23" x 31" piece of batting

1 yard of 17"-wide lightweight paper-backed fusible web

Assorted threads to match appliqué fabrics

Gold metallic thread for appliqué

Metallic needle (recommended)

Teflon pressing sheet (recommended)

Cutting

From the dark-blue batik, cut:
- 1 rectangle, 13" x 16½"

From the tan metallic print, cut:
- 1 rectangle, 5" x 13"
- 2 strips, 2¾" x 42"; crosscut into:
  - 2 strips, 2¾" x 22¼"
  - 2 strips, 2¾" x 18½"
- 8 squares, 1¾" x 1¾"
- 16 squares, 1¼" x 1¼"

From the dark-gold metallic print, cut:
- 3 strips, 2½" x 42"
- 3 strips, 1¼" x 42"; crosscut into:
  - 1 strip, 1¼"x 12½"
  - 2 strips, 1¼" x 20¾"
  - 2 strips, 1¼" x 14"
- 8 squares, 1¾" x 1¾"
- 4 squares, 1¼" x 1¼"

Creating the Center Panel

❶ Refer to "Fusible-Web Appliqué" (page 8) and use the patterns (pages 91–93) to prepare the individual appliqué pieces for the manger and letter sections of the wall-hanging center. Consult the materials list above and the photo (page 88) for fabric choices as needed. Preassemble the manger unit using the prepared appliqué pieces (see "Preassembling Appliqué Units" on page 9).

❷ Center the prepared manger appliqué unit approximately 1¼" from one short side of the dark-blue rectangle. Follow the manufacturer's instructions to fuse the unit in place.

❸ Center the prepared letters on the tan metallic 5" x 13" rectangle to spell *Rejoice*; fuse in place.

❹ Finish the raw edges of each appliqué piece using a machine blanket stitch, zigzag stitch, or satin stitch. Trim the manger section to 12½" x 16" and the letter section to 12½" x 4½".

❺ Sew the dark-gold metallic 1¼" x 12½" strip to the bottom of the manger section. Add the letter section to the bottom of the strip. Press the seam allowances toward the strip.

Making the Outer-Border Corner Blocks

❶ Draw a diagonal line from corner to corner on the wrong side of each tan metallic 1¾" square. Layer each marked square on top of a dark-gold metallic 1¾" square, right sides together. Sew ¼" from both sides of the marked lines. Cut the squares apart on the marked lines. Each pair of squares will yield two half-square-triangle units. Press the seam allowances toward the darker gold. Square up each unit to 1¼" x 1¼".

Make 16.

2 Lay out four half-square-triangle units from step 1, four tan metallic 1¼" squares, and one dark-gold metallic 1¼" square into three horizontal rows as shown. Sew the pieces in each row together. Press the seam allowances toward the squares. Sew the rows together. Press the seam allowances toward the top and bottom rows. Repeat to make a total of four corner blocks.

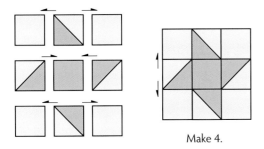

Make 4.

Adding the Borders

1 Refer to the wall-hanging assembly diagram at right to sew the dark-gold metallic 1¼" x 20¾" inner-border strips to the sides of the wall-hanging top. Press the seam allowances toward the borders. Add the dark-gold metallic 1¼" x 14" inner-border strips to the top and bottom of the wall-hanging top. Press the seam allowances toward the borders. The wall hanging should measure 14" x 22¼" in order for the outer border to fit.

2 Sew the tan metallic 2¾" x 22¼" outer-border strips to the sides of the wall-hanging top. Press the seam allowances toward the outer-border strips. Add a corner block to each end of the tan metallic 2¾" x 18½" strips. Press the seam allowances toward

the strips. Join these strips to the top and bottom of the wall hanging. Press the seam allowances toward the outer-border strips.

Wall-hanging assembly

Finishing the Wall Hanging

1 Prepare the backing so that it's 4" longer and 4" wider than the wall-hanging top.

2 Layer the backing, batting, and wall-hanging top; baste together.

3 Quilt as desired.

4 When the quilting is complete, square up the wall-hanging sandwich. Refer to "Binding" (page 12) to attach the binding using the dark-gold metallic 2½"-wide strips.

5 Add a hanging sleeve and a label to the back of the wall hanging.

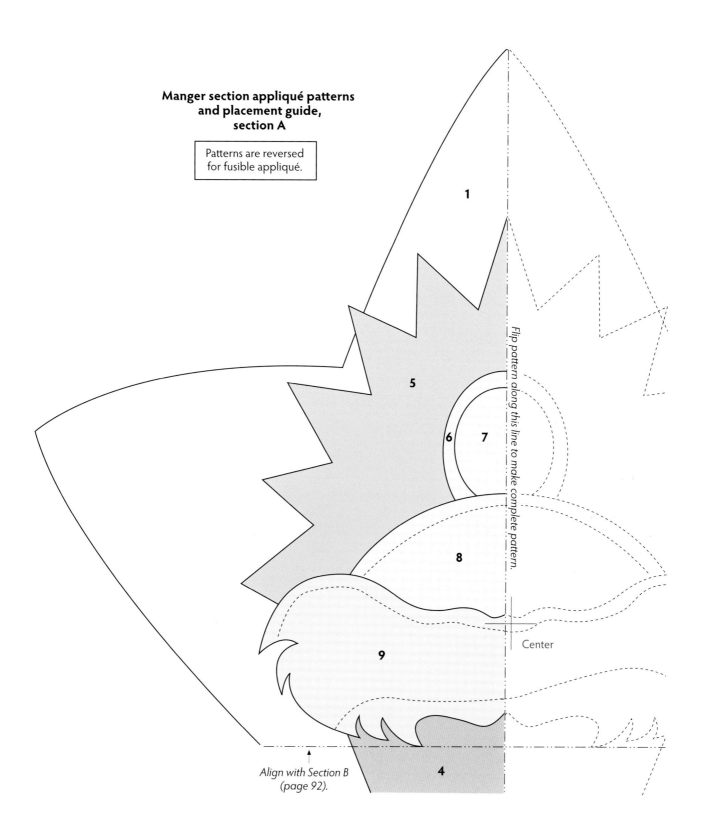

Manger section appliqué patterns and placement guide, section A

Patterns are reversed for fusible appliqué.

1

5

6 7

8

9

4

Flip pattern along this line to make complete pattern.

Center

Align with Section B (page 92).

**Manger appliqué patterns
and placement guide,
section B**

Patterns are reversed
for fusible appliqué.

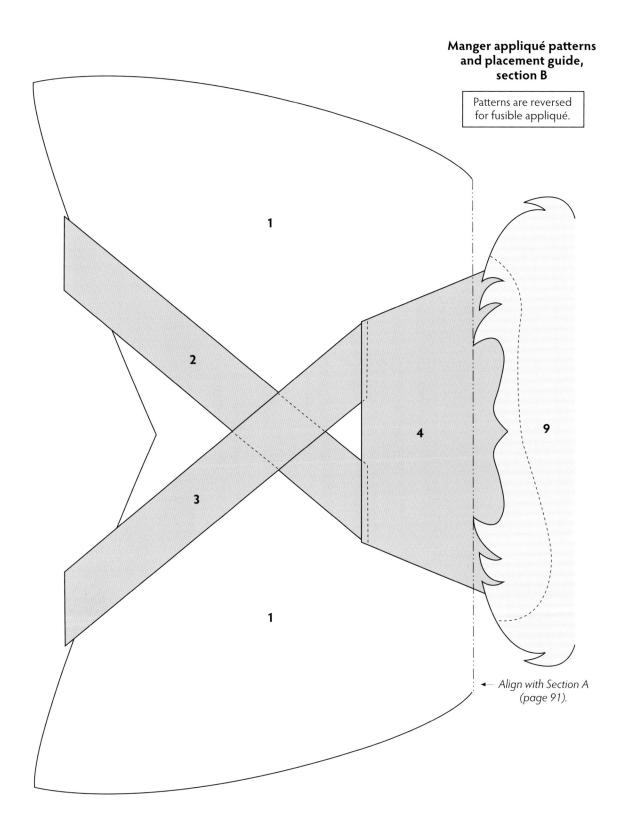

1

2

3

4

9

1

← *Align with Section A
(page 91).*

Letter section appliqué patterns

Patterns are reversed
for fusible appliqué.

Make 2 of letter "e" and
1 each of remaining letters.

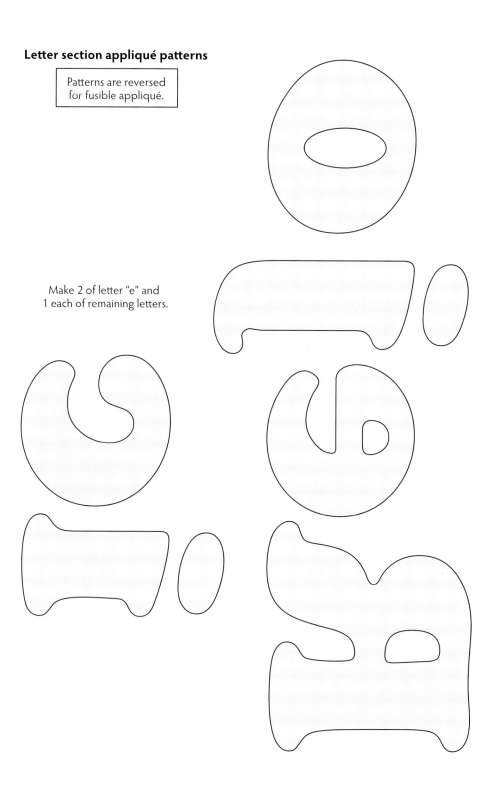

Acknowledgments

My deepest thanks are extended to the following people:

Ken Taylor, the world's best husband.

Mary Green, Karen Costello Soltys, Laurie Baker, Tiffany Mottet, Cathy Reitan, and the many people at Martingale who put my designs into print. Thank you for your faith in my ability and the opportunity to share my work with others.

Debbie Lindgren, for her encouragement and friendship.

Mary Kay Fields, for her friendship, advice, and last-minute bindings.

Marcia Biancone, Irene McErlain, Doris Zayacz, Jean Curasi, Nancy Leski, and the other "Quilters of Faith" of Western Hills Christian Church, for their inspiration and support.

Cheryl Winslow of Starshine Quilting, for her beautiful long-arm quilting.

Fred, Paul, Bob, Bea, Ellen, Peggy, Marilyn, Brad, and all the other terrific people at Pocono Sew & Vac, who keep my sewing machine running beautifully and provide me with great support.

Sandy Muckenthaler and Hoffman Fabrics, for providing me with beautiful Hoffman Bali fabrics.

About the Author

Cheryl Almgren Taylor is a teacher, designer, and author who specializes in fusible appliqué. She loves the creativity and possibilities the technique offers and likens it to her love of playing with paper dolls as a child.

Cheryl made her first quilt in 2000 and was immediately hooked. Having sewn from the time she was 13 years old, quilting was an easy transition. Very quickly she began designing her own quilts and her career as an author began in 2007 when Martingale published her Storybook Snuggler pattern series, featuring children's quilts designed around storybook themes. Since then she has authored two books, *Deck the Halls* and *Inspirational Appliqué,* and her work appears regularly in quilt publications. She also travels and teaches regionally and on a national level.

A native Californian, Cheryl grew up in the small oil town of Taft. She has been transplanted to New Jersey where she works as a teacher in public education. Her husband, Ken, is a pastor and she is active in their church where, in addition to other activities, she leads a quilting group. They are parents to three grown children and grandparents to seven amazing grandchildren.

Most of Cheryl's free time is spent in quilting pursuits, from meeting with her quilt group to shop hopping for new fabric. She also loves to read mystery novels and travel, especially to visit family.